Flexible Grouping in Reading

Practical Ways to Help All Students Become Stronger Readers

Michael F. Opitz

University of Southern Colorado

SCHOLASTIC
PROFESSIONAL BOOKS

NEW YORK • TORONTO • LONDON • AUCKLAND • SYDNEY

ACKNOWLEDGMENTS

I am greatly indebted to the many individuals who contributed to this manuscript: to Susan Womack Closset for her encouragement; to my university students who desired to know more about effective group practices; to Perry Rogers, a university student who formatted the lesson plan form on the computer; to teachers Mary Carter, Betty Cagle, Carol McGhee, Pat Funk, Sarah Adams, Susan Anderson, Brooke Coleman, Barbara VanGeystel, and Lou Grimes, whose contributions breathe life into many of the ideas expressed throughout the book; to reviewers Karen Sullivan and Joyce Baltas, whose suggestions helped to bring clarity; to the Scholastic staff—Terry Cooper, editor-in-chief, Wendy Murray, senior editor, and Linda Beech, editor—for their attention to detail; to Dr. John Ryan, director of the USC Center for Teaching, Learning & Research, for providing me with the time to write and, for her continued support in every conceivable way, I thank Sheryl, my first lady.

Cover design by Laurel Marx
Cover photo by Donnelly Marks
Interior design by Solutions by Design, Inc.
Interior Illustrations by Drew Hires
Interior photos on pages 9, 19, 65, and 93 by Catrina Genovese.
Photos on pages 49, 77, and 87 by Joan Beard.

ISBN 0-590-96390-2

Contents

Introduction 5

Chapter 1: Reflecting on Grouping Practices 9
   Ability Grouping and Flexible Grouping Defined. 10
   How Do Ability Grouping and Flexible Grouping Differ? 10
   Why Use Flexible Grouping? 13

Chapter 2: Getting to Know Students 19
   How Can We Learn About Students? 19
   Using What We Discover 45
   Meet Six Children 45

**Chapter 3: Understanding Flexible
Grouping Basics** 49
   Four Ways to Implement Flexible Grouping 50
   More Flexible Grouping Considerations 58

Chapter 4: Selecting Texts for Flexible Grouping 65
   What Is Grade Level? 66
   What Are Reading Levels? 66
   Guidelines for Selecting Books for Flexible Grouping 68
   Teaching Children to Choose Their Own Books 72
   Four Ways to Teach Book Selection 74

**Chapter 5: Planning for Successful Reading
Experiences in Flexible Grouping** 77
   Two Important Questions for Flexible Grouping 78
   Teaching Strategies 79
   Planning Groups so That All Children Can Succeed 80
   Classroom Scenario 83

Chapter 6: Checking Progress in Flexible Grouping 87

Assessing Individuals Within a Flexible Group 88

Keeping Track of Student Progress 89

Chapter 7: Looking at the Whole Program 93

Flexible Grouping in the Total Reading Program 93

Some Sample Schedules 96

A Few Reminders—for You—and Parents, Too! 99

Appendixes

A. How-to Explanations of Reading Strategies in
Flexible Grouping 105

B. Annotated Bibliography 119

References 125

Introduction

I'm convinced! Good fortune is sometimes disguised as misfortune. Take, for example, an experience I had a few years ago. After completing graduate studies, I worked as a reading specialist in an elementary school. Prior to my arrival, the staff had decided to teach children with additional learning needs within their classrooms rather than having the children leave the room to receive extra help. As part of this plan, specialists came into the classrooms and worked with the teachers and students. The staff had also been directed to use a newly adopted literature-based basal reading program.

The misfortune, or so I thought at the onset, was the curriculum director's misconception about reading instruction. Teachers were expected to have all students read the anthology designated for their grade level instead of having students read the text that corresponded to their actual reading performances. Recognizing that children needed "just right" material to gain the most from guided reading instruction, I questioned how teachers would be able to help children who had difficulty reading the designated grade-level text. How would teachers be able to meet students' needs if students weren't grouped according to their ability to read a given text?

My attempt to answer these questions was one good fortune in disguise. It led me to reexamine the research on ability grouping, which revealed the many problems associated with it. This reexamination helped me to seek out some alternatives to ability grouping—more flexible ways of grouping children—and different ways to engage children with a common grade level text so that all could experience success regardless of reading level.

A second good fortune was seeing what happened with the children. Watching children normally placed in the "low" group actively participate in whole-group, "on-grade-level" reading lessons showed me that despite their perceived reading levels, all students could contribute to one another's learning. Instead of being singled out, these students blended in with the rest of the class. One day, for example, a third-grade boy who had been identified as needing extra help participated in a group that was reading about seals. He was able to read most of the text, offered his ideas during the discussion, and volunteered to read two sentences orally to the group. His teacher commented, "You know, if someone had walked in here while we were doing this, she would have never known that there were kids struggling with reading."

Gratifying, to be sure, but the real clinchers came from the students. Halfway through a book, for example, Jamie looked up at me and, with a surprised look, said, "Hey! I didn't know I could read this!" She then continued reading. True, her reading was far from fluent, more like a cha-cha than a waltz. And yes, she struggled with some vocabulary. But she met with enough success to see herself as a reader, which kept her reading the book.

Another good fortune was working with a group of teachers willing to learn with me—teachers who were willing to take risks by trying some of my discoveries; teachers who were open to sharing their own discoveries and ideas; teachers who were committed to their own growth, to my growth, and to maximum growth for all students; courageous teachers. I have worked with numerous teachers since and have continued to share and learn more about flexible grouping and about techniques that help ensure successful reading.

This book is the result of a lengthy journey to understand better how to help all students reach their full reading potential through a variety of grouping strategies. My primary purpose is to assist those teachers who need some support in implementing flexible grouping. Indeed, this book consists of practical, kid-tested grouping options and teaching procedures that better enable all children to become stronger readers of all kinds of books.

To begin, you'll reflect on definitions related to grouping along with suggestions for ways to learn about your students. Just how best to group children comes next, and, as you'll see, there are several considerations to think through.

Selecting appropriate books is a big part of any reading program, and this holds true for flexible grouping. You'll read about ways to select books as well as ways to help children choose their own. Following this section, you'll find ideas for using these books for successful reading experiences.

Strategies for checking students' progress—important components of any teaching—come next. These are followed by a look at how flexible grouping fits into an entire reading program.

Two appendices bring the book to a close. The first contains a detailed description of teaching strategies, and the second includes an annotated bibliography for further reading. The articles and books in this bibliography are written by teachers who share how they use grouping options in their classrooms. As these teachers suggest, using a variety of grouping techniques requires patience and determination because ability grouping has been dominant in our schools for decades. Altering or deviating from this deeply ingrained structure by using flexible grouping can prove challenging. It will undoubtedly cause you to question and examine some of your assumptions about teaching, learning, and children in general. The challenge is well worth the effort, however, because, as Houser (1992) states, "It is only by regularly questioning the assumptions upon which we base our teaching that we can be responsive to the changes in our student populations, the materials we use, and the demands of our society for which schools function."

Using a variety of grouping strategies and different teaching strategies may make you feel unsure of yourself, wondering if you're doing anything "right." At these times, especially, keeping your focus on what it is you are trying to accomplish for all children will help. As Mary Carter, a third grade teacher, told me one day, "I don't know if we're doing everything right, but never before have we talked about the instruction for these kids so much!"

Firsthand experience has shown me that questioning and examining assumptions and replacing or augmenting yesterday's ideas with new ideas take time, courage, and energy. It's also shown me that children deserve all three.

CHAPTER 1

Reflecting on Grouping Practices

"The challenge for educators is to begin to see students in inclusive ways and to value diversity in their classrooms so that those students who have become a 'ghost' . . . can become contributors."

—C. Dudley-Marling and S. Stires

Grouping children to teach reading has been with us for so long that we may do so without fully understanding why. Ability grouping, in particular, is so much a part of reading instruction that it is often used with little attention to what it actually means and with a lack of awareness of the consequences. More recently, another term, *flexible grouping*, has come into use. Just what is ability grouping? What is flexible grouping? What are the differences between the two? Why do I advocate flexible grouping? Answering questions such as these lays the groundwork for more effective teaching of reading to all children. Let's begin with some definitions.

ABILITY GROUPING AND FLEXIBLE GROUPING DEFINED

When I think of ability grouping and flexible grouping, two things come to mind—concrete and sand. *Ability grouping* makes me think of working with concrete to build permanent foundations meant to withstand change. When I think of *flexible grouping*, I picture working with sand to form temporary castles that the tide will wash away.

In a more formal sense, *The Literacy Dictionary: The Vocabulary of Reading and Writing*, edited by Theodore Harris and Richard Hodges, provides these definitions to make a distinction between ability grouping and flexible grouping:

> **Ability grouping:** the placement of students according to similar levels of intelligence or achievement in some skill or subject, either within or among classes or schools; tracking; homogeneous grouping.

> **Flexible grouping:** allowing students to work in differently mixed groups depending on the goal of the learning task at hand.

HOW DO ABILITY GROUPING AND FLEXIBLE GROUPING DIFFER?

The definitions hint at one difference between ability and flexible grouping—the assumptions on which they are based. Clearly, each focuses on markedly different beliefs about teaching and learning, and each plays out differently in the classroom. Most often, for example, ability groups reflect children's overall reading achievement; those with similar achievement levels are placed together in one of three groups—high, medium, or low—to receive instruction.

In contrast, flexible groups fulfill a variety of purposes. All children needing to learn a specific skill, for example, might be grouped to learn that skill. After children have learned the skill, the group dissolves.

The following chart lists some of the major likenesses and differences between ability and flexible grouping. Use the chart to reflect on your own grouping practices. Where would you place yourself on each characteristic? You might also find the All Children Survey on page 12 helpful in analyzing your present approach.

> "Exposure to different points of view in interaction helps children to examine their environment more objectively and to use perspectives other than their own."
>
> —Elizabeth Cohen

Assumptions

Ability Grouping

- Literacy knowledge characterized by general achievement level. Children grouped by level so that the teacher can provide instruction appropriate for the group.
- Children must master a sequenced set of materials to progress from one level to the next.

Flexible Grouping

- Literacy knowledge characterized by several abilities. Children grouped in a variety of ways so that the teacher can provide appropriate instruction depending on the purpose for the group.
- All children can read grade-level texts regardless of "level" if provided the necessary support.

Grouping Procedures

Ability Grouping

- General achievement
- Static

Flexible Grouping

- Specific performance
- Fluid

Teacher Behaviors

Ability Grouping

- Groups are treated differently depending on perceived level.

Flexible Grouping

- Deliberate efforts are made to treat all groups similarly

Instruction

Ability Grouping

- Different groups receive different kinds of instruction with the "low" group receiving more lower-level tasks.
- Oral round-robin reading
- Different assignments for different groups

Flexible Grouping

- All groups are provided higher-order thinking activities.
- Much silent reading sometimes accompanied by purposeful oral reading exercises
- Use of open-ended assignments to provide for individual differences

Materials

Ability Grouping

- Prescribed sequence for all to follow
- Dominated by teacher selection

Flexible Grouping

- Variety of materials with an emphasis on reading whole books
- Student choice sometimes permitted

Assessment

Ability Grouping

- Commercial tests

Flexible Grouping

- Daily observations and performance on authentic tasks

Scholastic Professional Books, 1998

> "All children can learn in a system
> that respects their abilities."
> —C. Roller

**Observe your classroom and how you currently plan activities.
Read each statement and place a check in the appropriate column.**

Statement	Yes	No
1. All children are provided the same amount of time to read authentic books and/or stories throughout the day.		
2. All children spend the same amount of time on skill/drill work.		
3. All children are permitted to read without interruptions.		
4. All children are expected to solve problems when reading.		
5. All children are provided time to solve problems when reading.		
6. All children are provided the same amount of time to read books during guided reading instruction.		
7. All children are provided many "just right" books.		
8. All children are engaged with high-level questions.		
9. All children preread silently before reading orally before a group.		
10. All children appear to enjoy reading.		
11. All children have the opportunity to self-select books.		
12. All children are provided time to read independently.		

WHY USE FLEXIBLE GROUPING?

This is a reasonable—and important—question. Here are nine reasons for using flexible grouping that I have discovered as the result of my own teaching experiences over the past two decades and after much research on this topic. You may well think of additional reasons based on your own experiences.

Nine Reasons for Using Flexible Grouping

1 TO ENSURE THAT ALL LEARNERS FEEL PART OF THE COMMUNITY. By community, we might look at this useful definition: "A place in which students feel cared about and are encouraged to care about each other. They experience a sense of being valued and respected; the children matter to one another and to the teacher. They have come to think in the plural: they feel connected to each other; they are part of an 'us'" (Kohn 1996, 101).

> "The foundation of flexible grouping lies in the building of a sense of community. Realizing that they are valued and have a common purpose, students are better able to work with each other."
> —T. Gunning

As the definition relates to reading, then, children have opportunities to share like reading experiences and, as a result, feel connected to one another. Reading the same story or book, for example, provides students with a common text and ideas to share and discuss. As a result of listening to one another, students also see additional ways of interpreting text and thus gain new insights.

> "When we are valued for the human beings we are, we become less threatened by others, we feel safe, then we feel successful and accepted."
> —N. Zaragoza

First-grade teacher Susan Anderson says it this way: "When you have children ranging from mildly mentally handicapped to gifted in one room, it is important for each child to feel as much ownership of the material as possible. When a beginning reader holds, tracks, and reads the same material as a more experienced reader, the message is powerful. We don't all learn to read at the same pace, but there are many reading experiences from which we can share and learn. Using flexible grouping enables everyone to feel empowered."

The illustration shown here suggests one way to create this sense of community among readers. You begin by having the entire class participate with the same activity, proceed to flexible grouping (some type of small groups) that will best help

Whole Class / Small Flexible Groups

children to accomplish the daily objective, and finish with the whole class coming back together to share their experiences. (See Chapter 3 for more details.)

> "Only in small group discussions do students have the opportunity both to engage in extended conversation about complex ideas and to have their understandings deepened by the ideas of their peers."
> —K. Au, J. Mason, and J. Scheu

2 TO HELP CHILDREN BETTER UNDERSTAND WHAT THEY HAVE READ. Smaller, flexible groups make student participation more likely and afford opportunities to paraphrase, explain, and elaborate on a given text.

3 TO ENABLE STUDENTS TO WORK COOPERATIVELY WITH A WIDE VARIETY OF PEERS. By working cooperatively in flexible groups, students interact with others in the class that they wouldn't have otherwise. The research on cooperative learning points to the results: improved academic achievement and social relations (Johnson and Johnson 1987; Slavin 1988).

4 TO HELP STUDENTS FEEL MORE INVOLVED IN THEIR LEARNING. Interest is a major contributing factor in learning to read. In fact, children often read at a level that far surpasses their normal level when they read about a topic of interest (Anderson, Heibert, Scott, and Wilkinson 1985). One of the best ways to keep this interest alive, thereby engaging students and encouraging them to extend themselves as readers, is to allow them to form groups based on their interests rather than their abilities.

5 TO CAPITALIZE ON THE RESEARCH THAT SUPPORTS THE USE OF GROUPING AS A WAY TO ENGAGE STUDENTS WITH APPROPRIATE INSTRUCTION AND MATERIALS (Hallinan 1984; Karweit 1983; Cohen 1994). Children who read and engage in discussion have better attitudes toward reading and better gains in reading achievement than children who read but do not have this interaction (Manning and Manning 1984).

> "If we are serious about our goal to have all students love reading, ability groups would seem to be counterproductive."
> —R. Barr

6 TO OFFSET THE EFFECTS OF ABILITY GROUPING. The sole use of ability grouping has not proved advantageous, especially for those children placed in the "low" group. More specifically, research has shown the following:

○ *Ability grouping can have negative consequences for the children placed in the "low" group.* As the chart on page 17 shows, students in the low group are asked to perform low-level tasks. In addition, the very concept of a low group influences teacher and student behavior. In essence, a self-fulfilling prophecy emerges: Students are taught in a way that insures low performance. Students see themselves as low and perform according to their expectations. What's disturbing about these

Scholastic Professional Books, 1998

consequences is that most often we as teachers are not conscious of them. Awareness of these consequences enables us to promote positive chan es.

- *Ability grouping is based assumptions.* One
  assumption is that child be grouped by ability. A second
  assumption is that, once gr ped, teachers can improve instruction by devoting all of their time and energy planning lessons for an entire "homogeneous" group instead of devising several different lessons.

> "Labels may affect not only how children think of themselves but also how they are perceived by others."
>
> —L. Spear-Swerling and R. Sternberg

While these assumptions may sound right at first, both become suspect upon reflection. Researchers have noted that innate ability is difficult to determine (Gamoran 1992; Allington and Cunningham 1996). Instead, children are really grouped according to their achievement, either measured or perceived. Say, for example, that all children are given a reading test composed of two parts—comprehension and vocabulary—and that the test reveals a total score. The total score is often used to group children, but a close look at individual performances may reveal that the total score was achieved in different ways. One student may score well in comprehension but show a weakness in vocabulary. A second student may score poorly in comprehension but do well in vocabulary. These two students have different needs but may be placed in the same "homogeneous" group because of their overall score. Depending on the focus of the group, one child may have difficulty. In other words, some differentiated instruction must occur if all children are to be successful. Most often, one plan does not suffice. Flexible grouping is needed.

> "Perhaps the most important and difficult task for those who would change tracking is to confront deeply held beliefs, such as the belief that academic ability is fixed early and is largely unchangeable or that achievement differences can be largely accounted for by differences in ability."
>
> —J. Oakes

- *Children placed in a "low" group get the opposite of what they need.*
  After researching the effects of ability grouping, Barr (1995) concluded that children in low groups receive inferior instruction when compared to children in high groups. For example, children in the low reading group in first grade are so placed because they have limited experiences with language. Because we know that children learn language by using it, they need to be immersed in activities with print, such as journal writing, shared reading, and listening to stories read aloud. However, more often than not these children receive instruction that emphasizes just the opposite—isolated skill instruction.

- *Ability grouping often sorts children by social class*
  (Allington and Cunningham 1996; Shannon 1985; Gamoran 1992). Children from economically deprived homes are often

> "Students reading at a given level do not all have the same strengths or weaknesses nor do they learn best in the same ways."
>
> —A. Harris and E. Sipay

Scholastic Professional Books, 1998

less exposed to the rich literacy background so important to emerging readers. As a result, these students are often put in low reading groups and offered a "slowed-down curriculum" (Allington and Cunningham 1996). The result? These children fall farther behind while students in the "high" groups continue to advance.

7 TO HELP THE MAJORITY OF STUDENTS BY USING TIME EFFICIENTLY. By grouping three children who need to learn the same strategy, you can teach the strategy once rather than three different times.

8 TO PROVIDE FOR INDIVIDUAL DIFFERENCES USING OPEN-ENDED ASSIGNMENTS. Open-ended assignments, those that children can complete at their own level, enable teachers to provide for individual differences while maintaining sanity; such assignments are manageable. They also allow *all* students much time on task! Finally, open-ended assignments can take many forms, thus permitting students to use different intelligences to show understanding. When a class uses literature logs, for example, all students may be expected to write a prediction before they begin reading. All can also respond to a story in some way in these logs. True, some students spell words conventionally whereas others do not. And yes, some use more elaborate sentences than others. However, the advantage to this type of assignment is that it provides *all* students with an opportunity to apply what they know. Regardless of "level," therefore, all are challenged.

> "All children are entitled to the same literacy experiences, materials, and expectations."
> —S. Walmsley and R. Allington

Here's an example: To set the stage for reading *Big Max* by Kin Platt, I had students create a clue folder using construction paper. Students folded the paper in half, made a paper magnifying glass, and attached it to the folder cover. When reading the book, students recorded clues that they believed would help Big Max discover who had stolen Jumbo, a prize elephant. As a culminating activity, all students completed the story map related to this book. The example on the left shows how one reader, who had been identified as needing additional help, completed these tasks.

As the example illustrates, the use of open-ended tasks makes it more likely that all children are exposed to the same type of literacy experiences. All learners in the classroom come to realize that they have some commonalities regardless of "level."

STORY MAP

Title: Big max
Author: By Kin plaH

Setting: in the city
Characters: king Big max
Place: in the coshrey
Time: log time ago

Problem: the problem was judoma was lost and ne dont no were he was.

Events Leading to Resolution:
1. they call Big Max and He send I will be ther
2. And tle fling ther
3. And they look for Him
4. And Big Max sied Happe Birthday to bnams

Resolution: They found joud play with his friend.

Scholastic Professional Books, 1998

Unintended Consequences of Ability Grouping: Research-Based Generalizations Concerning "Low" Readers

Consequence	Research Documentation
TASKS	
Low-ability readers:	
• Spend more time in oral round-robin reading and reading workbook assignments.	Allington 1977, 1983; Leinhardt, Zigmond, and Cooley 1981
• Receive more isolated skills and drills.	Allington 1983; J. Collins 1986; R. Haskins, T. Walden, and C. Ramey 1983
• Receive fewer comprehension activities.	Allington 1983
• Have fewer opportunities to read and write.	Allington 1983, 1984; Stanovich 1986
TEACHER BEHAVIORS	
• Allow more outside interruptions for low-ability groups	Allington 1980; McDermott 1976; Eder 1981, 1982
• Devote twice as much time to decoding instruction and practice	Allington 1980; DeStephano, Pepinsky, and Snaders 1982; Gambrell, Wilson, and Gnatt 1981
• Interrupt low readers more often when they miscue	Allington 1980
• Emphasize discipline and behavior more often than academic learning	Oakes 1994
• Gear instruction toward dependence rather than independence	Allington 1983
• Demonstrate lower levels of enthusiasm, preparation, and expectations	Gamoran 1992
• Have children wait longer to receive instruction and concluding activities than on reading instruction itself	Leinhardt, Zigmond, and Cooley 1981; McDermott 1976
• Tend to make few changes in group membership after the first month of school so that students, beginning in first grade, remain placed in their bottom groups throughout their schooling and rarely learn to read and write up to grade level	Allington 1983; Shannon 1985; Weinstein 1976; Barr and Dreeben 1991
• Ask questions that do not expect students to use high levels of thinking	Seltzer 1976
STUDENT BEHAVIORS	
• By spring of a school year, children in low-ability groups show three times as much inattentive behavior as children assigned to high-ability groups;	Felmee and Eder 1983
• Have lowered academic expectations;	Eder 1983; Hiebert 1983
• Have lowered self-concepts;	Eder 1983; Hiebert 1983; Mann 1960; Oakes 1992
• Feel excluded from class activities and often find classmates to be unfriendly;	Oakes 1994
• Are more apathetic;	Oakes 1994
• Spend less time on task;	Gambrell, Wilson, and Gnatt 1981; Beckerman 1978; Haskins, Waldin, and Ramey 1983

9 **TO ACCOMPLISH THE GOALS OF A READING PROGRAM AND ADDRESS NATIONAL READING AND LANGUAGE ARTS STANDARDS.** An effective reading program has established goals, and they are often in concert with the IRA/NCTE English language arts standards (1996). For example, the eleventh standard states: "Students participate as knowledgeable, reflective, creative, and critical members of a variety of literacy communities." This standard relates to the goals that a group of teachers and I developed for our reading program (see page 78).

Clearly, the use of flexible grouping better ensures that all students become stronger readers. Grouping children by general achievement alone is not enough.

> "Imagine what would happen if we viewed every mind as a source of genius."
> —A. Wheelock

Scholastic Professional Books, 1998

CHAPTER 2

Getting to Know Students

"Ideally, each teacher should be a master at observing student behavior and assessing each child's reading."

—R. Farr and R. Carey

No question about it—it takes time to know students. Just as we need to use various approaches to teach children, we must also use a variety of ways to understand them. For it is only in recognizing students' strengths and weaknesses that we can effectively use flexible grouping to help them. This chapter provides some suggestions.

HOW CAN WE LEARN ABOUT STUDENTS?

By watching them! Observations provide a wealth of information. Sometimes, observations are unstructured with no specific purpose other than to get a feel about how children function within a classroom. At other times, observations are very directed because they have a particular goal.

Other informal measures also help to guide observations and provide ways to document information about children's reading. Choosing the best measures can appear an awesome task because there are so many from which to choose! In addition to the questions in the chart below, I have found these three questions to be helpful:

- What do I want to know?

- Why do I want to know it?

- How can I best discover it?

The chart on page 22 shows some ways to answer these questions. The main idea is that we need to use the tool that will best help us discover what it is we want to know at a given time. Pages 21–45 provide reproducible assessment forms and directions for their use. You may want to adapt them to meet the needs of your students.

CONCEPTS ABOUT PRINT AND PRINT SETTINGS

- To what extent does the student attend to print?

- How does the student handle books?

- Does the student expect the print to make sense and have personal meaning?

- How does the student use information from the print setting?

USE OF STRATEGIES

- How does the student handle the information-giving systems of language? Does the reader use a flexible strategy that includes language cues (syntactic, semantic, and graphophonic) to construct meaning, or does the reader rely on a single cueing system?

- Does the student monitor his or her reading by asking, "Am I making sense of what I am reading?"

- Does the reader self-correct when the flow of language and meaning is interrupted?

- Is there a dialect or first language influence on the student's reading, and how does the student handle this influence?

- What strategies does the reader use to approach suitable but unfamiliar text?

- What strategies does the student use when he or she comes to an unknown word?

READING FLEXIBILITY

- Does the student read at the same speed regardless of the material?

- Does the rate vary with purpose of reading?

- Does the student ever use skimming, scanning, and/or reading for detail?

Sources: Watson 1985, 119–120; Rhodes and Dudley-Marling 1989

FLEXIBLE GROUPING IN READING • GETTING TO KNOW STUDENTS

Scholastic Professional Books, 1998

TIP: *Practical Assessments for Literature-based Reading Classrooms* by Adele Fiderer (Scholastic, 1995) offers a wealth of additional ideas that will help you get to know children.

How to Use the Reproducibles

Independent Reading Record (see page 28)

1. Reproduce the form for each student.

2. Use the chart to help you determine the genres a child is reading. Simply write the code next to each title in the column Type of Book. Have students keep records of the books they read during independent reading time.

3. After students have recorded five or more books, analyze the titles to see the type(s) of books they are reading. Use the code at the bottom of the page or develop a code more suitable for your students.

4. Teach students how to use the code. Doing so will not only assist your analysis but also will help students identify their own interests.

Primary Reading Survey (Grades 1 and 2) (Fiderer 1995; see page 29)

1. Provide students with copies of the Primary Reading Survey.

2. Read each statement and give students time to circle the face that best tells how they feel about the statement.

3. Count the circled faces to discover a child's attitude about reading. A majority of smile faces indicates a positive attitude toward reading, a majority of sad faces suggests the opposite.

Reading Attitude Survey for Grades 3 and Up (Johns 1997; see page 30)

1. Make copies of the reproducible for each student.

2. Explain that you will read each statement. You might say something like this: "I am going to read you each statement you see on the paper. Circle the letter that best tells how you feel about this statement."

3. Read each statement, pausing long enough for students to circle the appropriate letter.

4. Score and interpret the results. Use the following code:
   SA = 1; A = 2; U = 3; D = 4; SD = 5.

   Items 1, 3, 4, 6, 8, 9, 11, 12, 13, 16, 17, and 20 are considered negative attitudes toward reading. Items 2, 5, 7, 10, 14, 15, 18, and 19 are considered positive attitudes toward reading. Add the points for the positive and negative statements. Scores above 60 indicate a positive attitude toward reading.

The What, Why, How of Assessment

WHAT do I want to know?	WHY do I want to know it?	HOW can I best discover it?
What does the child choose to read?	To become good readers, children need to read many different kinds of books. I want to see what they are choosing so that I can help to round out their reading experiences.	Independent Reading Record (see page 28)
How does the student feel about reading?	Attitude has a big impact on the ability to read a text. Identifying attitudes will help me see if I need to help a child develop a more positive approach, thereby making reading a more enjoyable experience. Children with a positive attitude are more likely to attempt reading for a variety of purposes.	Primary Reading Survey (see page 29) Reading Attitude Survey for Grades 3 and Up (see page 30)
What are the reader's interests?	Identifying interests will help me to select books for instruction and the classroom library. I can also use these interests to group children in different ways, enabling them to get to know many of their peers.	Interest Inventory (see page 31)
How does the student view reading?	Faulty perceptions of what it means to read can inhibit reading growth. Uncovering these ideas can help me to see which are accurate and those that need to be altered.	Student Interview (see page 32)
What are the child's reading levels?	Children need to read books of varying difficulty if they are to become strong readers. A majority of what they read should be at their independent and instructional levels. If text is beyond these levels, I need to choose teaching strategies that will provide the child with enough support to read the text.	Running Record (see page 33) Informational reading inventories such as Johns' *Basic Reading Inventory*
What background does the child bring to a text?	Background knowledge is essential for interacting with text. Children who have the background for a text are better able to recall and summarize what they have read.	Prediction Task (see page 35)
How well does the student comprehend?	Comprehension is the essence of reading. I need to directly teach children who lack strategies for comprehending text.	Retelling (see page 36)

Scholastic Professional Books, 1998

WHAT do I want to know?	WHY do I want to know it?	HOW can I best discover it?
What strategies does the child use when reading?	Good readers use a variety of strategies to assist them. Relying on one or two strategies to the exclusion of others can prevent growth. I want to make sure that students can use different strategies to ensure their independence.	Student Interview (see page 32) Running Record (see page 33) Modified Miscue Analysis (see page 37)
Does the child have an understanding of how print functions?	Understanding how print functions and knowing the terminology associated with reading are essential for beginning readers. Identifying what the child knows and what the child needs to learn can help me to prevent confusion.	Print Concepts (see page 38)
Does the child have phonemic awareness?	Phonemic awareness appears to be a good predictor of reading success. It is also a precursor to phonics instruction. I need to make sure that all children have this awareness before I provide instruction that will cause misunderstandings.	Test of Phonemic Awareness (see page 40)
What word identification strategies does the child use?	The ability to use what is known about letters and sounds to decode words is the essence of phonics instruction. I need to make sure that a child is applying what is known. I also need to know if the child is developing a store of sight words to facilitate fluent reading.	Names Test (see page 41) Basic Word List (see page 44)

Interest Inventory (see page 31)

1. Provide each student with an Interest Inventory form.

2. Set aside time for students to complete the form, offering assistance when necessary. Or have students fill out this form with your help during brief individual conferences.

3. Tally the results on a matrix. List students' names down the left side and the reading interests across the top. Place a [✔] in the space given if the child indicates that this is a reading interest.

4. Use the chart to select books and magazines for your classroom library.

Student Interview (see page 32)

1. Make a copy of the Student Interview Guide for each student.

2. Each interview will take approximately ten minutes. In a one-on-one con-

Scholastic Professional Books, 1998

ference, ask each question. Because this is an unstructured interview, the questions may be asked in any order. Some questions may need to be reworded. However, the only prompt that can be given is, "Anything else?"

3. Interpret the results. Questions 1, 2, and 3 are designed to elicit perceptions of reading. Questions 4, 5, 6, and 7 elicit strategies used in reading. Do answers to the first three questions primarily focus on reading as a meaning-seeking activity? Do the responses primarily focus on reading as an act of calling, or simply saying, words? Do the responses focus on something other than understanding or word calling? Do the responses to questions 4–7 show that the reader has a limited set of strategies? Again, you might find a matrix helpful. List students' names down the left and their perceptions/strategies across the top. This will help you to see how students are alike and different and who needs to learn a broader repertoire of strategies as well as who needs to develop an accurate view of reading as understanding.

Running Record (adapted from Clay 1993; see page 33)

1. Choose an appropriate text, one that is between 50 and 100 words.

2. Make copies of the Running Record.

3. Explain the procedure to the child: "I would like to listen to you read today. While you are reading, I am going to take some notes to help me remember how you read."

4. Have the child read the book. While the child is reading, make the following notations:

   - Make a ✔ [check] for each word read correctly.

   - Write and circle any word that is omitted.

   - Add a ^ [caret] for any word that the child inserts. Also write the word.

   - Write and draw a line through any word that is substituted and write what the child said in its place.

   - Draw an arrow back to where the child repeats.

   - Write SC when the child self-corrects.

   - Write TA if you assist with the word.

   - For each self-correct and/or error, mark the type of cue(s) that was used by writing M (meaning cue), S (structure cue), V (visual cue) and circling the letter to show which was used.

5. Summarize the results on the Running Record Summary. (See page 34.)

6. Finish with a retelling (see page 36) to assess comprehension.

Scholastic Professional Books, 1998

Prediction Task (see page 35)

1. Provide the student with a story to read.

2. Ask the student to read the title of the story.

3. After the title has been read, say something like: "Based on your reading of the title, what do you think this story will be about?"

4. Use the form to record the student's predictions and your assessment of them.

Retelling (adapted from Irwin and Mitchell; see page 36)

1. Ask the student to silently read a specific story.

2. Ask the student to retell everything that he or she can remember. You might say something like: "Tell me everything you can remember about the story. Pretend you are telling it to a friend who has never heard it."

3. As the student retells the story, use the Retelling form to record how well the child retells. Use prompts such as "What comes next?" only if necessary. If you give prompts, make sure you indicate this by writing "Assisted" on the form.

Modified Miscue Analysis (adapted from Fiderer; see page 37)

1. Choose an appropriate text. Although a formal miscue analysis requires 400 words or more, a passage of fewer words, say 150, is acceptable here. The passage should be long enough to help you see if and how the child uses different strategies during reading. You may want to use passages from an informal reading inventory such as John's *Basic Reading Inventory*. Make a copy for the child and another for yourself.

2. Make copies of page 37 and the Retelling record on page 36.

3. Explain the procedure to the child: "I would like to listen to you read so that I can hear what you do when you read. I am going to take notes as you read."

4. As the child reads, make the following notations on your copy of the passage:

   ○ Circle any word that the child omits.

   ○ Add a ^ [caret] for any word that the child inserts. Write the inserted word.

   ○ Draw a line through any word that is substituted. Write the substituted word.

   ○ Write a C on the word if the child self-corrects.

   ○ Note repetitions by writing R and drawing a line back to where the child repeats.

○ Do not make marks for words read correctly.

5. Have the child do a retelling to check comprehension. Record your assessment on the retelling form.

6. Now you are ready to analyze the child's reading using the Modified Miscue Analysis. Here's what you do:

   ○ Write each miscue and the text that should have been read. Remember that self-corrects and repetitions are not counted as miscues.

   ○ For each miscue, ask the three questions on the form. If the answer is yes, circle the appropriate letter(s): M, S, V.

7. Answer these questions in the spaces on the form:

   ○ How often does the student self-correct?

   ○ Which cues are used most often?

   ○ How well was the child able to comprehend the story?

   ○ Was the reading fluent? choppy?

   ○ Were there a lot of repetitions? If so, what caused them?

   ○ Does the child attend to punctuation?

8. Based on your analysis, determine what you think the child needs to learn.

Print Concepts (Adapted from Clay 1993; Gillett and Temple 1994; see page 38)

1. Choose a book that is relatively short, such as *The Hungry Man* by Phyllis Root.

2. Make a copy of the Print Concepts form and follow the directions.

3. Summarize your observations on the Summary of Print Concepts form.

Test of Phonemic Awareness (Yopp 1995; see page 40)

1. Make copies of the form.

2. Individually, ask children to read the words as directed on the form. Be sure that students say the sounds, not the letters.

3. Score the words as directed. Remember, the child must segment the entire word in order to receive credit for the word. That is, partial credit is not given.

4. Use the following to determine degrees of phonemic awareness:

   ○ All or almost all items segmented = Phonemically aware

   ○ Some items segmented = Emerging phonemic awareness

• Few or no items segmented = Lacking in phonemic awareness

Names Test (Duffelmeyer, Krose, Merkley, and Fyfe 1994; see pages 41–43)

1. Make two copies of the Names Test and one copy of each Scoring Matrix.

2. Give the Names Test the student and ask him or her to read aloud the names. Keep a copy for yourself.

3. As the child reads each name, write exactly what the child says above each name on your copy of the Names Test.

4. To analyze the child's performance:

   • Locate each mispronounced name on the test.

   • Find these names on the scoring matrix and circle the phonic elements that were mispronounced.

   • Count the circled elements for each category.

   • Record the total number of errors on the bottom of the test.

Basic Word List (Adapted from Johns, 1997; see page 44)

1. Print on a card each word shown on the Basic Word List.

2. Make copies of the Basic Word List to record what each child does when looking at the word cards.

3. Say something like: "Today I want to find out which of these words you know."

4. Show the child one word at a time. Write down what the child says on the form. Continue until the child shows signs of frustration or miscalls several words.

5. Note that this form can be used at the end of each quarter. Use a different color to record the results for each quarter.

Scholastic Professional Books, 1998

Name_____

INDEPENDENT READING RECORD

Title	Author	Date Finished	Type of Book

CODE:

F = fiction	B = biography	PL = play
NF = nonfiction	M = myth	C = collection
PB = picture book	FT = folktale	P = poetry

Name_____

PRIMARY READING SURVEY

How do you feel when:	😊	😐	☹️
1. your teacher reads a story to you?			
2. your class has reading time?			
3. you can read with a friend?			
4. you read out loud to your teacher?			
5. you read out loud to someone at home?			
6. someone reads to you at home?			
7. someone gives you a book for a present?			
8. you read a book to yourself at home?			

How do you think:

9. your teacher feels when you read out loud?			
10. your family feels when you read out loud?			

How Do You Feel About How Well You Can Read?

Make this face look the way you feel.

Adapted from Practical Assessments for Literature-Based Reading Classrooms by Adele Fiderer, Scholastic Professional Books, 1995.

Name_____

Reading Attitude Survey for Grades 3 and Up

Directions: The 20 statements that follow will be read to you. After each statement is read, circle the letter that best describes how you feel about that statement. Your answers will not be graded because there are no right or wrong answers. Your feeling about each statement is what's important.

SA = Strongly Agree   A = Agree   U = Undecided
D = Disagree   SD = Strongly Disagree

SA   A   U   D   SD   **1.** Reading is for learning but not for enjoyment.

SA   A   U   D   SD   **2.** Money spent on books is well spent.

SA   A   U   D   SD   **3.** There is nothing to be gained from reading books.

SA   A   U   D   SD   **4.** Books are a bore.

SA   A   U   D   SD   **5.** Reading is a good way to spend spare time.

SA   A   U   D   SD   **6.** Sharing books in class is a waste of time.

SA   A   U   D   SD   **7.** Reading turns me on.

SA   A   U   D   SD   **8.** Reading is only for students seeking good grades.

SA   A   U   D   SD   **9.** Books aren't usually good enough to finish.

SA   A   U   D   SD   **10.** Reading is rewarding to me.

SA   A   U   D   SD   **11.** Reading becomes boring after about an hour.

SA   A   U   D   SD   **12.** Most books are too long and dull.

SA   A   U   D   SD   **13.** Free reading doesn't teach anything.

SA   A   U   D   SD   **14.** There should be more time for free reading during the school day.

SA   A   U   D   SD   **15.** There are many books that I hope to read.

SA   A   U   D   SD   **16.** Books should not be read except for class requirements.

SA   A   U   D   SD   **17.** Reading is something I can do without.

SA   A   U   D   SD   **18.** A certain amount of summer vacation should be set aside for reading.

SA   A   U   D   SD   **19.** Books make good presents.

SA   A   U   D   SD   **20.** Reading is dull.

From *Improving Reading: A Handbook of Strategies,* Second Edition by Jerry L. Johns and Susan Davis Lenski. Copyright © 1994, 1997 by Kendall/Hunt Publishing Company. Used with permission.

FLEXIBLE GROUPING IN READING • GETTING TO KNOW STUDENTS
Scholastic Professional Books, 1998

Name _____ Date _____

Please ✔ the right spaces to help me get to know you!

1. Do you like to read?

_____ yes _____ sometimes _____ no

2. What kinds of books do you like to read? (√ as many as you want!)

_____ animal _____ science _____ true

_____ make-believe _____ about people _____ science fiction

_____ mysteries _____ poetry _____ funny

_____ series _____ myths _____ folktales

_____ plays _____ riddles/jokes _____ books with pictures

_____ scary stories _____ books that tell how to make things

3. Who is your favorite author? _____

4. What is your favorite book? _____

5. What book would you like to read? _____

6. What magazines do you like to read?

_____

7. Which do you like best?

_____ hardcover books _____ softcover books

Why? _____

_____

8. What helps you to choose a book to read?

_____

_____

_____

Name _____ Date _____

1. What is the most important thing about reading?

_____

_____

2. When you are reading, what are you trying to do?

_____

_____

3. What is reading?

_____

_____

4. When you come to a word you don't know, what do you do?

_____

_____

5. Do you think it's important to read every word correctly? Why? Why not?

_____

_____

6. What makes a person a good reader?

_____

_____

7. Do you think good readers ever come to a word they don't know? If yes, what do you think they do?

_____

_____

Name _____   Date _____

RUNNING RECORD

Title of Book _____   Author _____

Page	Reading Performance	Errors M S V	Self-Corrects M S V
		TOTALS	

M = Meaning Cue   S = Structure Cue   V = Visual Cue

Scholastic Professional Books, 1998

Name _____ Date _____

RUNNING RECORD SUMMARY

Title of Book_____ Author_____

Summary of Reading Performance

Total # of Words _____   Total # of Errors _____   % of accuracy _____

Reading Level (Circle the one that matches the % of accuracy.)

95%–100% = Independent   90–94% = Instructional   89% or lower = Frustration

Total # of Self-Corrections _____   Self-Correction Rate 1:_____

NOTE: Self-correction rates of 1:3, 1:4, or 1:5 are good. Each ratio shows that the reader is attending to discrepancies when reading.

- -

Summary of Observations

1. What did the reader do when unknown words were encountered? (✔ all that apply)

    _____ made no attempt

    The reader made an attempt in these ways:

    _____ asked for help   _____ looked at pictures

    _____ used letter/sound knowledge   _____ used meaning

    _____ used structure (syntax)   _____ tried again

    _____ skipped it and continued reading _____ looked at another source

2. How often did the reader attempt to self-correct when meaning was not maintained?

    (Circle one.)   always   frequently   sometimes   seldom   never

3. When the reader did self-correct, which cues were used? (✔ all that apply.)

    _____ letter/sound knowledge (visual)   _____ meaning   _____ syntax (structure)

Calculating Accuracy Rate

1. Subtract the total # of errors from the total # of words in the text to determine the number of words that were correctly read.

2. Divide the number of words correctly read by the number of words in the passage to determine % of accuracy.

    EXAMPLE: 58 total words – 12 errors = 46 words read correctly

    46 words read correctly ÷ 58 total words = 79% accuracy

Calculating Self-Correction Rate

Use this formula: $\dfrac{\text{self-corrections} + \text{errors}}{\text{self-corrections}} = 1:\underline{\quad}$

Based on Clay, 1993, and Morrison, 1994; adapted by M. Opitz.

Name _____ Date _____

PREDICTION TASK

Book or Story Title _____

Author _____

Prediction Based on Title _____

_____

_____

_____

Reasons Given _____

_____

_____

_____

_____

Check all that apply:

_____ Student drew on prior knowledge of topic.

_____ Student drew on personal experience.

_____ Student guessed wildly.

_____ Student used word meaning.

_____ Student was familiar with author.

_____ Student guessed creatively.

Background Knowledge for Title (Place the student on this continuum.)

|⊢——————————————————|——————————————————⊣|
little   some   much

FLEXIBLE GROUPING IN READING • GETTING TO KNOW STUDENTS
Scholastic Professional Books, 1998

Name_____

RETELLING

Directions: Indicate with a check the extent to which the reader's retelling includes or provides evidence of the following information.

Retelling	None	Low	Moderate	High
1. Includes information directly stated in text.				
2. Includes information inferred directly or indirectly from text.				
3. Includes what is important to remember from text.				
4. Provides relevant content and concepts.				
5. Indicates attempt to connect background knowledge to text information.				
6. Indicates attempt to make summary statements or generalizations based on text that can be applied to the real world.				
7. Indicates highly individualistic and creative impressions of or reactions to the text.				
8. Indicates affective involvement with the text.				
9. Demonstrates appropriate use of language (vocabulary, sentence structure, language conventions).				
10. Indicates ability to organize or compose the retelling.				
11. Demonstrates sense of audience or purpose.				
12. Indicates control of the mechanics of speaking or writing.				

Interpretation: Items 1–4 indicate the reader's comprehension of textural information; items 5–8 indicate metacognitive awareness, strategy use, and involvement with text; items 9–12 indicate facility with language and language development.

Source: Adapted from Pi A. Irwin and Judy N. Mitchell

MODIFIED MISCUE ANALYSIS

Miscue Record of _____ Grade _____

Title and Pages _____ Date _____

- **M** = Meaning. Does the miscue make sense?
- **S** = Sentence structure. Does the sentence sound right?
- **V** = Visual. Does the miscue look like the word?

Student	Text	Cues Used
		M S V
		M S V
		M S V
		M S V
		M S V
		M S V
		M S V
		M S V
		M S V
		M S V

Strategies Used _____

_____

Comprehension _____

_____

Fluency _____

_____

Needs to Learn... _____

_____

Adapted from Practical Assessments for Literature-Based Reading Classrooms by Adele Fiderer, Scholastic Professional Books, 1995.

Scholastic Professional Books, 1998

Name _____ Date _____

PRINT CONCEPTS

Title of Book _____

Directions: Using the book that you have selected, give the following prompts to encourage the child to interact with it. Read the story aloud as you proceed. Place a √ next to each item answered correctly.

Prompt	Response (✔ = correct)	Print Concept
1. Hand the child the book upside down, spine first, saying something like: "Show me the front of this book." Then read the title to the child.		layout of book
2. Say: "I would like to begin reading the story, but I need your help. Please open the book and point to the exact spot where I should begin reading."		print conveys message
3. Stay on the same page and say: "Point to where I need to start reading."		directionality: where to begin
4. Say: "Point to where I should go after I start reading."		directionality: left-to-right progression
5. Say: "Point to where I go next." Read the pair of pages.		directionality: return sweep
6. Turn the page and say: "Point to where I should begin reading on this page. Now point to where I should end. " Read the page.		terminology: beginning and end
7. Turn the page and say: "Point to the bottom of this page. Point to the top of it. Now point to the middle of it." Read the page.		terminology: top, bottom, middle
8. Using the same page, say: "Point to one letter."		terminology: letter
9. Again using the same page, say: "Point to one word."		terminology: word
10. Turn the page. Make sure that this page contains words that have corresponding upper- and lowercase letters. Read the pages. Then point to a capital letter and say: "Point to a little letter that is like this one."		matching lower to uppercase letters
11. Turn the page and say: "Let's read these pages together. I'll read and you point." Read the pages.		speech to match print
12. Finish reading the book. Then turn back to a page that has the punctuation marks you want to assess. Point to the punctuation mark and say: "What is this? What is it for?"		punctuation: period, question mark, quotation marks

FLEXIBLE GROUPING IN READING • GETTING TO KNOW STUDENTS
Scholastic Professional Books, 1998

Name _____ Date _____

SUMMARY OF PRINT CONCEPTS

Title of Book _____

Directions: Use this form to summarize your observations of print concepts.

Observations

The child demonstrates knowledge of the following print concepts (√ the appropriate spaces)

_____ layout of books (item 1)

_____ print contains written message (item 2)

_____ directionality (items 3, 4, 5)

_____ terminology associated with reading (items 6, 7, 8, 9)

_____ uppercase letters (item 10)

_____ lowercase letters (item 10)

_____ speech to print match (item 11)

_____ punctuation (item 12)

Comments/Notes

_____

_____

_____

_____

_____

_____

_____

_____

_____

_____

_____

_____

_____

_____

Scholastic Professional Books, 1998

TEST OF PHONEMIC AWARENESS

Directions: Tell the child: "Today we're going to play a word game. I'm going to say a word, and I want you to break the word apart. You are going to tell me each sound in the word in order. For example, if I say *old* you should say /o/l/d/." Stress that the child should say the sounds, not the letters. Give these items as practice and assist as necessary: *ride, go, man*.

Circle the items on the test that the student correctly segments. Record incorrect responses on the line after each item.

1. dog _____   **12.** lay _____

2. keep _____   **13.** race _____

3. fine _____   **14.** zoo _____

4. no _____   **15.** three _____

5. she _____   **16.** job _____

6. wave _____   **17.** n_____

7. grew _____   **18.** ice _____

8. that _____   **19.** at _____

9. red _____   **20.** top _____

10. me _____   **21.** by _____

11. sat _____   **22.** do _____

Comments/Notes

_____

_____

_____

_____

_____

_____

Adapted from H. Yopp, 1995. *The Reading Teacher* 49 [1]: 20–9.

FLEXIBLE GROUPING IN READING • GETTING TO KNOW STUDENTS
Scholastic Professional Books, 1998

Name _____ Date _____

THE NAMES TEST

Jay Conway	Tim Cornell	Chuck Hoke	Yolanda Clark
Kimberly Blake	Roberta Slade	Homer Preston	Gus Quincy
Cindy Sampson	Chester Wright	Ginger Yale	Patrick Tweed
Stanley Shaw	Wendy Swain	Glen Spencer	Fred Sherwood
Flo Thornton	Dee Skidmore	Grace Brewster	Ned Westmoreland
Ron Smitherman	Troy Whitlock	Vance Middleton	Zane Anderson
Bernard Pendergraph	Shane Fletcher	Floyd Sheldon	Dean Bateman
Austin Shepherd	Bertha Dale	Neal Wade	Jake Murphy
Joan Brooks	Gene Loomis	Thelma Rinehart	

Phonics Category	Errors	Total Possible
Initial consonants	_____	/37
Initial consonant blends	_____	/19
Consonant digraphs	_____	/15
Short vowels	_____	/36
Long vowels/VC–final e	_____	/23
Vowel digraphs	_____	/15
Controlled vowels	_____	/25
Schwa	_____	/15

The Names Test from Duffelmeyer, Frederic A., Kruse, Anne E., Merkley, Donna J., & Fyfe, Stephen A. (October, 1994) *The Reading Teacher*, 48(2), 118-129. Copyright © 1994 by the International Reading Association. All Rights reserved.

Scoring Matrix for Names Test, Part 1

Name	InCon	InConbl	ConDgr	ShVow	LngVow/VC-e	VowDgr	CtrVow	Schwa
Anderson				A			er	o
Austin						Au		i
Bateman	B				ate			a
Bernard	B						er, ar	
Bertha	B		th				er	a
Blake		Bl			ake			
Brewster		Br					ew, er	
Brooks		Br				oo		
Chester			Ch	e			er	
Chuck			Ch	u				
Cindy	C			i	y			
Clark		Cl					ar	
Conway	C			o		ay		
Cornell	C			e			or	
Dale	D				ale			
Dean	D					ea		
Dee	D					ee		
Fletcher		Fl	ch	e			er	
Flo		Fl			o			
Floyd		Fl				oy		
Fred		Fr		e				
Gene	G				ene			
Ginger	G			i			er	
Glen		Gl		e				
Grace		Gr			ace			
Gus	G			u				
Hoke	H				oke			
Homer	H				o		er	
Jake	J				ake			
Jay	J					ay		
Joan	J					oa		
Kimberly	K			i	y		er	
Loomis	L					oo		i
Middleton	M			i				o
Murphy	M		ph		y		ur	

InCon = Initial Consonant   LngVow/VC-e = Long Vowel/Vowel Consonant–final e
InConBl = Initial Consonant Blend   VowDgr = Vowel Digraph
ConDgr = Consonant Digraph   CtrVow = Controlled Vowels
ShVow = Short Vowel   Schwa = Schwa

The Names Test from Duffelmeyer, Frederic A., Kruse, Anne E., Merkley, Donna J., & Fyfe, Stephen A. (October, 1994) The Reading Teacher, 48(2), 118-129. Copyright © 1994 by the International Reading Association. All Rights reserved.

SCORING MATRIX FOR NAMES TEST, PART 2

Name	InCon	InConbl	ConDgr	ShVow	LngVow/VC-e	VowDgr	CtrVow	Schwa
Neal	N					ea		
Ned	N			e				
Patrick	P			a, i				
Pendergraph	P		ph	e, a			er	
Preston		Pr		e				o
Quincy				i	y			
Rinehart	R				ine		ar	
Roberta	R				o		er	a
Ron	R			o				
Sampson	S			a				o
Shane			Sh		ane			
Shaw			Sh				aw	
Sheldon			Sh	e				o
Shepherd			Sh	e			er	
Sherwood			Sh			oo	er	
Skidmore		Sk		i			or	
Slade		Sl	ade					
Smitherman		Sm	th	i			er	a
Spencer		Sp		e			er	
Stanley		St		a		ey		
Swain		Sw				ai		
Thelma			Th	e				a
Thornton			Th				or	o
Tim	T			i				
Troy		Tr				oy		
Tweed		Tw				ee		
Vance	V			a				
Wade	W				ade			
Wendy	W			e	y			
Westmoreland	W			e			or	a
Whitlock			Wh	i, o				
Wright					i			
Yale	Y				ale			
Yolanda	Y			a	o			a
Zane	Z				ane			

InCon = Initial Consonant   LngVow/VC-e = Long Vowel/Vowel Consonant–final e
InConBl = Initial Consonant Blend   VowDgr = Vowel Digraph
ConDgr = Consonant Digraph   CtrVow = Controlled Vowels
ShVow = Short Vowel   Schwa = Schwa

The Names Test from Duffelmeyer, Frederic A., Kruse, Anne E., Merkley, Donna J., & Fyfe, Stephen A. (October, 1994) *The Reading Teacher*, 48(2), 118-129. Copyright © 1994 by the International Reading Association. All Rights reserved.

Name_____

BASIC WORD LIST

First Quarter:	Date:	Score:
Second Quarter:	Date:	Score:
Third Quarter:	Date:	Score:
Fourth Quarter:	Date:	Score:

Directions: Place a ✔ next to the word if the child reads it correctly. If the child mispronounces the word, write what the child says. If the child does not know the word and says so, write DK (Don't Know).

Word	Child's Response	Word	Child's Response
1. the		11. for	
2. of		12. you	
3. and		13. he	
4. to		14. on	
5. a		15. as	
6. in		16. are	
7. is		17. they	
8. that		18. with	
9. it		19. be	
10. was		20. at	

Adapted from Johns,' 1997

USING WHAT WE DISCOVER

How can we use the information we have about children to form flexible groups? Here are two suggestions:

1 **RECORD INFORMATION ON AN INDIVIDUAL RECORD FORM SUCH AS THE ONE ON PAGE 46.** A form like this shows how readers change over a year.

2 **COMPILE INFORMATION ON A MATRIX.** I'll admit it! I like matrices. Why? Because they reveal so much information—information that can be used to form flexible groups with ease. Take, for example, the Concepts About Print matrix on page 54. Pat Funk, a first-grade teacher, was able to form several groups to teach specific concepts by looking at this one chart.

MEET SIX CHILDREN

Children have a way of breathing life into every corner of the classroom. It's no different with this book—a classroom of sorts. Here, then, is a brief introduction to six children who will resurface throughout the book in various flexible groups. Five of the children are third graders, one is a first grader, and all are actual students with whom I have worked. All are "first timers"—none has been retained in any grade. Names have been changed for confidentiality.

Jamie, a first grader

Jamie is a very quiet girl. She never speaks unless called on, and even then, especially in large groups, she sometimes does not respond. She appears to be interested in pets, and she has a horse and a cat at home. Jamie knows the names of some letters but is lacking in phonemic awareness. Likewise, she knows some concepts about print but has several still to learn. Jamie likes to be read to, and retellings show that her comprehension is strong. One activity that Jamie especially enjoys is art. She is always drawing or painting and uses art as a way of communicating in her journal.

Bill, a third grader

According to his father, reading has been hard for Bill since the very beginning. A recent running record revealed that his current instructional level is equivalent to an ending first grader, his independent level is of a beginning first grader, and second-grade material is frustrational. Both Bill's oral and silent reading are painfully slow. His oral reading is halting, with many substitutions, repetitions, and long pauses. Most of Bill's miscues are significant, and he rarely self-corrects. He appears to have few strategies for identifying unknown words and relies on asking as his primary strategy. Bill's comprehension is excellent, however, as is evidenced by his retellings and

Name_____

INDIVIDUAL READING RECORD

Characteristics	Date _____ Observations	Date _____ Observations	Date _____ Observations
Genres Read			
Attitudes			
Interests			
Views of Reading			
Reading Levels			
Comprehension			
Reading Strategies			
Other			

Scholastic Professional Books, 1998

story discussions. This might be attributable to his rich background, a result of frequent travel. Bill doesn't appear to enjoy reading and would spend all of the independent reading time just looking for books if allowed to do so. Bill says that his purpose for reading is to get finished as fast as he can; he notes that his mom is a good reader, meaning that she reads quickly. Bill likes science a lot.

Kamal, a third grader

Kamal is a very fluent reader who is able to read just about every kind of text in the room. He has a large reading vocabulary and uses many effective strategies when he comes to unknown words. He self-corrects when meaning is disrupted. Kamal also listens well, and responses in his literature log show that he is able to decipher main ideas from what he reads. Class discussions also indicate that Kamal interacts with the reading material. He has a wide variety of interests such as baseball, animals, and science-related topics. Although he will read several different kinds of books, Kamal gravitates toward nonfiction. According to a recent assessment, his independent level is fifth grade, and his instructional is fourth.

Rosa, a third grader

Rosa loves to read books that are chosen by the teacher and shows all attributes of being a good reader. She self-corrects when she needs to and uses several strategies such as skipping an unknown word and coming back to it later. Rosa is especially good at articulating—orally and in writing—main ideas gleaned from what she has read. Her oral reading provides an excellent model of fluency. Based on her last reading of graded passages, her instructional level is third grade. When asked about the purpose of reading, Rosa says that a person has to understand what the words are saying. During independent reading, she tends to gravitate toward books about horses. Expanding her choices would provide Rosa with opportunities to learn about other topics that she might find interesting.

Brenda, a third grader

Although Brenda has a limited reading vocabulary, she is fairly adept at listening to others and articulating main points. Her instructional reading level is approximately second grade. Brenda uses few strategies when reading and rarely predicts what she thinks might occur in a story. Her main strategy when encountering an unknown word is to sound it out. She appears to enjoy books about animals in general, dogs in particular, and she spends most of the independent reading time with books about them.

Matt, a third grader

Matt is competitive and sees most every reading experience as a race. He can recall most words but guesses wildly at those he doesn't know and con-

Scholastic Professional Books, 1998

tinues reading even when the guessed word makes no sense. When reading silently, Matt always tries to be the first one finished and reads only part of each page to ensure that this is the case. His comprehension is weak, according to retellings. When talking about reading, Matt mentioned that the most important thing was to say the words. Perhaps it is this misconception that is causing him difficulty. Matt does choose to read, however, and he spends the majority of independent reading time reading rather than selecting. He especially likes mysteries and scary stories. Matt's instructional level appears to be right at second grade.

CHAPTER 3

Understanding Flexible Grouping Basics

"Using grouping effectively requires teachers to be acute observers of the children in their classrooms, to listen to the children interact within groups and, most important, to listen to the children's own observations about the groups in which they participate."

—M. Heller

This chapter focuses on the answers to three important questions about flexible grouping:

- In what ways can groups be flexible?

- What is the optimum size for flexible groups?

- How often should the groups change?

FOUR WAYS TO IMPLEMENT FLEXIBLE GROUPING

Groups can be flexible in a number of ways and for a variety of purposes. I discuss four important aspects of flexibility in this chapter. Keep in mind that each is of equal value and that you can use any combination that works for you.

> "Problems arise when one grouping format becomes the sole or only context for literacy instruction. . . .The goal is to create particular contexts for students so they have opportunities to become proficient in particular literacy functions."
> —E. Heibert

1 **USE A VARIETY OF GROUPING TECHNIQUES.** Whatever grouping technique you use should support the purpose for reading. When the group's objective has been met, the group dissolves. As Karen Sullivan, a second-grade teacher at George Washington Elementary School in Mount Vernon, New York, says, "Membership is always open and rotating."

The chart on page 51 shows eight techniques for forming flexible groups. The following text provides brief classroom scenarios for each grouping option and shows how the children introduced in Chapter 2 are accommodated.

Classroom Scenarios for Flexible Grouping Techniques

Random To help students get to know one another and to develop listening and speaking skills, Betty Cagle, a third-grade teacher, chose five different colored markers and wrote student's name on an index card. She used each color five times. She then gave the name cards to the students and had them form groups according to the color used to write their name. Once in a group, students told about themselves—a like, dislike, a hobby, and their favorite kind of soda. Kamal was able to complete this activity with ease, as listening was one of his strengths.

Achievement Mary Carter and I wanted to have all third graders learn the characteristics of folktales. We had already determined each student's overall instructional reading level and decided that for this particular unit we would find folktales written at the students' levels to provide each with an opportunity to develop fluency. We grouped the students into one of four instructional reading groups. We gave each group member a folktale to read. Regardless of the folktale, all students were expected to complete the same activities. For example, all students contributed to a class matrix (see page 84) by choosing a group member to write the name of the folktale on the chart and place an X under every characteristic that was evident in the folktale. Brenda met with the children who read *The Elves and the Shoemaker,* as this folktale was written at her instructional level.

FLEXIBLE GROUPING TECHNIQUES

Grouping Technique	How	Use when . . .	Example
Random	This is completely arbitrary; have students group themselves by like titles or by given colors.	Placement is primarily for management and forming groups of equal size. Also good to use when you are trying to get students to know one another.	Students choose a title from a bag you circulate and group themselves by like title. There are enough titles to form groups of equal size.
Achievement	Use performance on a reading measure; students with similar scores are placed in the same group.	You want students to read literature selections at their instructional levels as determined by the reading measure.	When completing a folktale unit, students are directed to read a folktale that corresponds to their general reading levels.
Social (cooperative)	Group students according to specific social skills: leaders, followers; heterogeneous in that each has different skills.	Students need to function in different roles; students learn different roles from one another and work together to complete a group task.	Students read a script and glean important information to share with the class. When preparing, one person reads, another takes notes, another draws. One child is the group spokesperson.
Interest	This group is based on an interest survey. Assign students to a group or have them assign themselves to a group based on interest in a topic.	Student interest is the main motivating force for learning about a topic.	Students who are interested in a favorite author or illustrator come together to learn more about him or her.
Task	Those who are successful in completing given types of activities are grouped together.	You want to enable students to use their strongest modality to show understanding.	Children who find drawing enjoyable are grouped together to construct scenery for the reenactment of a story.
Knowledge of subject	Students with knowledge of a given subject or hobby are grouped together.	You want students to see likenessses among one another and share information.	Students who are interested in baseball cards are grouped together to share the statistics of their favorite players.

Scholastic Professional Books, 1998

Grouping Technique	How	Use when . . .	Example
Skill/strategy	Students lacking in a skill or strategy are grouped together.	You want to teach the skill or strategy to those who need to learn it.	Children who need to learn specific print concepts are grouped to learn them.
Student Choice	Students are allowed to group themselves according to a like characteristic such as author or genre.	You want to use literature response groups in which students take the lead; also good to use when student success is not dependent on choice.	Several books are displayed and students are invited to choose the book they would like to read. Those with like titles are then put in the same group.

Social (Cooperative) Brooke Coleman, a fifth-grade teacher, wanted to have all of her students learn about Spanish explorers. She decided to put children into groups of three according to their strengths. She gave each group reading material for a different explorer. Each member had a specific role to perform. The reader read the information orally while the rest of the group listened. The note taker recorded notes as the group members discussed what had been read and agreed on the most important details to share with the rest of the class. A third member presented the information to the class.

Interest Carol McGhee wanted to provide her third graders with a chance to learn about their favorite authors or illustrators. She asked students to indicate some of their favorite authors and illustrators by holding up books as reminders. She then gave students time to write the name of at least three favorites. Students who listed the same authors or illustrators were grouped together to complete various activities. Matt met with those who wanted to learn about Tomie dePaola because he, like the other group members, was interested in this author.

Task After her students read *Tikki Tikki Tembo* by Arlene Mosel, Pat wanted to have her first graders show understanding by dramatizing it. She randomly assigned students to groups by passing out the roles of main characters from the story, including the narrator. Classroom observations had revealed four students who were especially talented in using art to show their understanding of a story. These students had consistently drawn pictures to show main events or to recall details. Because she wanted to have a background for the dramatizations, Pat grouped these students together, instructing them to put as many details as they could remember in the scenery. Jamie was in this group.

Knowledge of Subject Betty wanted her third graders to become more comfortable working with one another while keeping the focus on reading. She asked students to think about their hobbies and/or interests and to write them down, listing their favorite first. She then collected the lists and grouped students accordingly. Bill joined the students who were interested in baseball because he had an extensive baseball card collection. Although Bill had difficulty reading material used in third grade, he was able to read the baseball cards with ease and could spout off numerous details about each of his favorite players. In fact, Bill also could teach others in the group how to read the cards.

Skill/Strategy Pat wanted to learn what her first-grade students knew about print concepts. She administered the Print Concepts reproducible to each student and made a class matrix to compile the results. (See page 54.) The matrix shows that Pat placed a circle next to the names of children who needed to learn a concept. A √ indicated children who already used the strategy. Pat designed specific lessons to teach the concepts, grouped the children according to their needs, and taught the lessons. Jamie was in a group for three days with Paul, Mica, Andrew, Jose, and Brandon because all of them needed to learn more about word-by-word matching. Pat reinforced these group lessons from time to time by calling on Jamie or one of the others to point to words when the class read a big book in unison.

Student Choice Carol wanted to have all twenty-four of her third graders do an author study of Beverly Cleary. Because she wanted to have six groups of four, Carol obtained four copies of six different titles written by Cleary. After doing a brief book talk to "sell" each book, she displayed them and gave each student an index card. Students wrote their name on the card and listed their first, second, third, and fourth choices. Carol collected the cards and put them into a paper bag. She then drew each card, one at a time, from the bag. As students' cards were drawn, they chose the book they had listed as their first choice. If the first choice was already taken, students took their second choice and so on until every child had a book. Students then formed groups by like titles. Rosa was in the group reading *Ramona and Her Mother*.

2 **USE TEACHING PROCEDURES THAT WILL BEST HELP ALL CHILDREN READ THE TEXT.** Some readers need more support than others when attempting to read a specific text. How much support they need depends on the text, the learners, and the overall reading experience you want to provide.

As part of a unit on weather study, for instance, Betty and I wanted her whole third-grade class to read *An Interview With a Meteorologist* by George Porter. Prior to selecting the story, we used a set of graded passages to

> "No one learns well while feeling afraid and ashamed."
> —L. Calkins

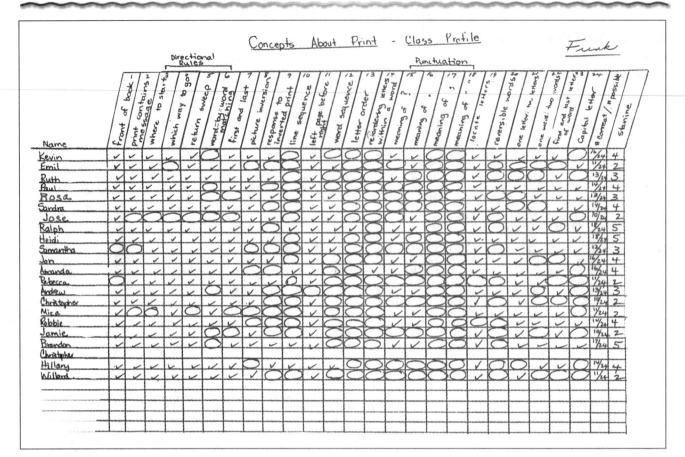

Pat's Profile tracks children's developing knowledge of print concepts.

estimate each student's instructional reading level. Thus, we knew that the interview would be challenging for some of the students, just right for the majority, and easy for a few. We wanted to choose a teaching procedure (see Chapter 5 for more about these procedures) that would best help all children read the text. We chose pairing students because the text was set up as an interview. One student could take the easier role of interviewer while the other student could read the more difficult role of meteorologist.

In the book, the interviewer's questions involve less text, so we gave this role to students with limited reading vocabulary such as Bill. We assigned the part of Mr. Dreumont, the meteorologist, to more fluent readers such as Kamal. With this flexible approach, less fluent readers were able to "save face" when reading with more fluent readers because their roles determined the amount and difficulty of the reading. Also, the more fluent readers provided excellent models for their partners.

3 USE DIFFERENT GROUPING PATTERNS WITHIN A GIVEN LESSON.
Perhaps the best way to provide support for all learners, accomplish your objective, and build a sense of community is to use more than one grouping option within a single lesson. Third-grade teacher Carol McGhee and first-grade teacher Susan Anderson provide good examples.

CONCEPTS ABOUT PRINT: CLASS PROFILE

Name	Directionality					Terminology						Punctuation
	1	2	3	4	5	6	7	8	9	10	11	12
	layout of books	print conveys message	where to begin	left-to-right progression	return sweep	beginning, end	top, bottom, middle	letter	word	upper and lower case matching	speech-to-print match	period, question mark, quotation marks

Scholastic Professional Books, 1998

Carol: 1 Book, 4 Cooperative Groups

Carol wanted her third graders to read *The Chocolate Touch* by Patrick Catling for several reasons. She felt that all her students would enjoy it and find it of high interest. She wanted to build a sense of community with the class and to show that students could all read the same text and learn from one another. Carol also wanted to use the book as a catalyst for a lesson on comparison/contrast, a skill listed in the third grade standards-based language arts curriculum. Finally, Carol wanted to teach students how to write questions using key terms, another skill in the curriculum.

Carol decided to form heterogeneous cooperative groups of six students each. Kamal and Rosa were in the same group because each had different strengths that would complement the other's. While Kamal's strength was fluency, Rosa's was the ability to articulate main ideas.

Carol began by having the groups brainstorm the names of candy they liked. She then had each group report on its favorites while she wrote the names on a large chart. Next she read the book title to the class and asked students to make predictions about the story. Carol wrote these on a chart and explained that she would revise it as students proceeded through the book. She then read the first chapter aloud. Students discussed the chapter and revisited their predictions to see if they needed to be changed. Once finished, students worked individually to write the name of the book's main character and their first impressions of him in literature logs. Later, they shared with the whole class what they had written.

Carol then conducted a 10-minute class lesson on writing questions, each beginning with a key term such as *what, why, where.* As she wrote each word on the board, Carol asked students to think of a question about the first chapter that began with one of the terms. She wrote their suggestions on the board. As you will learn later in this chapter, students returned to their groups to continue reading the book.

Susan: 1 Book, 3 Random Groups

Susan Anderson wanted all of her students to read *Who Took the Farmer's Hat?* by Joan Nodset. She started by reading the book to the whole class. She wanted to read with every child but had only eight copies of the book. Her solution? She randomly assigned the children to one of three groups

Susan's Rotation Schedule

Group	9:00–9:15	9:15–9:30	9:30–9:45
1	Guided Reading	Wordplay	Listening
2	Listening	Guided Reading	Wordplay
3	Wordplay	Listening	Guided Reading

FLEXIBLE GROUPING IN READING • UNDERSTANDING FLEXIBLE GROUPING BASICS

Scholastic Professional Books, 1998

and set up three center tasks. One of these was guided reading, when she would read with the children. Each group rotated through the centers following a schedule.

After students had rotated through the schedule, Susan led the whole class in a choral reading of the book, which she had printed on large pieces of chart paper.

4 USE A VARIETY OF READING MATERIALS. Often, flexible grouping involves the use of varied materials. Sometimes several different titles related to one topic are more appropriate for your lesson purpose and your students. For example, Carol wanted all of her third graders to read about animals. At the library she collected books about animals that were written on different levels. She also found children's publications such as *Ranger Rick* and *Zoobooks*. Carol labeled three tables in the back of her room, 1, 2, and 3. She displayed materials of varying reading levels on each table. As students entered the classroom, Carol gave them each a number.

Students selected books from the table that corresponded with their number. This numbering enabled all students to choose at once without unnecessary chaos. It also provided students with the opportunity to select material they felt they could handle comfortably. Carol then passed out guidelines for an animal report and provided students with time to complete their reports over the next week. As a culminating activity, students displayed their projects and went around the room looking at their classmates' work during a "gallery walk."

Animal Report

1. Choose an animal. Check with Mrs. McGhee since only two people may report on the same animal (wild animals, not pets).

2. Go to the library to learn about the animal. Use books, encyclopedias, and the vertical file. You may use the public library, too.

Write a 1/2 page report.

Tell where the animal lives,
    what it looks like,
    what it eats.

Tell if it is a mammal, bird, reptile, amphibian, or fish.

4. Draw a picture of the animal.

Extra Credit:

1. Make a map showing where the animal lives.

2. Make a drawing of the animal's track.

3. Make a diorama with the animal in its surroundings.

4. Make a book report.

Carol provides her students with some guidelines. Sharing guidelines helps all students succeed in writing their reports.

MORE FLEXIBLE GROUP CONSIDERATIONS

Size

Group size varies depending on purpose. However, I have found that groups of four work best. Each student has ample opportunity to engage in the learning or task at hand. Nevertheless, larger groups of up to six are common in many situations because of the number of students in a class. Larger groups can work but require closer monitoring to make sure that all students participate.

Duration

How often do flexible groups change? Recently, a colleague and I had a troubleshooting session about this issue:

> *Colleague:* I tried using flexible grouping, and I really had a hard time with it.
>
> *Me:* What did you find most difficult?
>
> *Colleague:* Without a doubt, it was trying to make sure that the groups changed every day and that the kids worked with different classmates every day.
>
> *Me:* Why did you change groups every day?
>
> *Colleague:* You mean I didn't have to?
>
> *Me:* Not really.

And so the conversation continued. *Change the groups when they are no longer needed.* The length of time that students need to be in a group varies. As Heller (1995) says, "Flexibility in grouping means that the group setting varies, sometimes daily, and depends on the objective of the lesson and individual needs of students."

As you may recall, Betty and I paired students like Kamal and Bill to read about the meteorologist. When students finished the story, we dissolved these paired groups; they were no longer needed because we had accomplished our goal for this particular reading lesson. Here are three other ways that teachers formed, used, and dissolved flexible groups.

Mary's Folktale Unit: 4 Days

When Mary and I formed groups for our folktale unit, we kept the achievement groups intact, Monday through Thursday. This time period enabled us to meet our primary objective —to provide "just right" reading material for students so that they could develop reading fluency while learning about folktales. On Friday, we invited students to choose a folktale that one of the other groups had presented on Thursday. This provided students

58

with an opportunity to learn from others. It also made clear to students that groups do indeed change. Brenda, who was in group 1, and her friend Sally, in group 4, read *The Monkey and Crocodile* by Paul Galdone together. In this case, Sally provided Brenda with the necessary support to read through the text.

The chart on page 60 shows the daily schedule each group followed during our one-hour reading period. Notice that regardless of general achievement level, all students were expected to read and respond to text in the same way. All were provided with an opportunity to learn to read by reading. What the schedule doesn't show is what we did the preceding Friday to prepare for the week's schedule. That day, we introduced the unit by reading a folktale, pointing out the characteristics of folktales, and explaining how students would be grouped for the week.

The folktale schedule shows what the whole class does during a one-hour reading period while the teacher facilitates what's happening in all groups and provides help where needed. However, if you want to give a small group more focused instruction, be sure the other students are doing meaningful activities. Using learning centers is one way to organize this type of instruction. If using learning centers is new to you, you'll find specific management tips in Opitz (1994).

Carol's *Chocolate Touch* Groups: 2 Weeks

Carol, the third-grade teacher who had her class read *The Chocolate Touch*, provides an outline of how she continued with the book after that first Monday. It shows yet another time frame for keeping children in the same group.

On Tuesday, Carol started with the whole class. She shared the grouping chart (see page 61) so that students could see where they fit into the overall plan and when they would be reading with her. Carol explained that the name in the cell is the group leader. She also told students that their groups would remain the same until the book had been read. She then gave students their literature log assignment and indicated which type of question to write for the chapter.

Procedures in place, Carol gave students time to get into their groups, talk with one another about the previous chapter, make a prediction for the day's assignment, and begin reading independently. When they finished reading, students responded in their literature logs, wrote their question, and, if other group members were still reading, read another self-selected book until all were finished and ready for discussion. When the groups completed their assigned reading and other activities, Carol brought them back as a whole class for sharing their thoughts and discussing their impressions of the main character.

Students followed this pattern for each subsequent day. On Friday of the second week, they participated in a review activity to culminate their read-

Scholastic Professional Books, 1998

GROUPING BY ACHIEVEMENT: FOLKTALE SCHEDULE

Group	Monday	Tuesday	Wednesday	Thursday	Friday
1	1. Read *The Three Wishes or The Elves and the Shoemaker.* 2. Fill in the class matrix.	1. Read *The Three Wishes or The Elves and the Shoemaker.* 2. Fill in the class matrix.	1. Choose one of the folktales you read. 2. Create a story map for your folktale. 3. Begin designing a scene that you will use to "sell" your folktale to others.	1. Continue designing your scene. 2. Present your folktale to the rest of the groups.	Your choice! Folktales read by all groups are displayed on the tables in the back of the room. 1. Choose any folktale you wish to read. 2. Choose the way you want to read it (partner, alone, follow along with a tape-recorded version). 3. Read several!
2	1. Read *Sticks, Stones or Ghost Catcher.* 2. Fill in the class matrix.	1. Read *Sticks, Stones or Ghost Catcher.* 2. Fill in the class matrix.	1. Choose one of the folktales you read. 2. Create a story map for your folktale. 3. Begin designing a scene that you will use to "sell" your folktale to others.	1. Continue designing your scene. 2. Present your folktale to the rest of the groups.	Your choice! Folktales read by all groups are displayed on the tables in the back of the room. 1. Choose any folktale you wish to read. 2. Choose the way you want to read it (partner, alone, follow along with a tape-recorded version). 3. Read several!
3	1. Read *Shepherd's Treasure or The Monkey and Crocodile.* 2. Fill in the class matrix.	1. *Read Shepherd's Treasure or The Monkey and Crocodile.* 2. Fill in the class matrix.	1. Choose one of the folktales you read. 2. Create a story map for your folktale. 3. Begin designing a scene that you will use to "sell" your folktale to others.	1. Continue designing your scene. 2. Present your folktale to the rest of the groups.	Your choice! Folktales read by all groups are displayed on the tables in the back of the room. 1. Choose any folktale you wish to read. 2. Choose the way you want to read it (partner, alone, follow along with a tape-recorded version). 3. Read several!
4	1. Read *Why Mosquitoes Buzz in People's Ears or Mufaro's Beautiful Daughters.* 2. Fill in the class matrix.	1. Read *Why Mosquitoes Buzz in People's Ears or Mufaro's Beautiful Daughters.* 2. Fill in the class matrix.	1. Choose one of the folktales you read. 2. Create a story map for your folk tale. 3. Begin designing a scene that you will use to "sell" your folktale to others.	1. Continue designing your scene. 2. Present your folktale to the rest of the groups.	Your choice! Folktales read by all groups are displayed on the tables in the back of the room. 1. Choose any folktale you wish to read. 2. Choose the way you want to read it (partner, alone, follow along with a tape-recorded version). 3. Read several!

FLEXIBLE GROUPING IN READING • UNDERSTANDING FLEXIBLE GROUPING BASICS
Scholastic Professional Books, 1998

COOPERATIVE GROUPING: Chocolate Touch SCHEDULE

Group	Tuesday	Wednesday	Thursday	Friday	Monday	Tuesday	Wednesday	Thursday
1: Angela Alex Bryce Christa Elisa Erin	Teacher led	Independent Angela	Independent Alex	Independent Bryce	Independent Christa	Independent Elisa	Teacher led	Independent Erin
2: Carl Chris Hermie Iris Jaynee Katharynne	Independent Carl	Teacher led	Independent Chris	Independent Hermie	Independent Iris	Independent Jaynee	Independent Kathy	Teacher led
3: Jason Jeff M. Josh C. Kersten Tanya Jude	Independent Jason	Independent Jeff	Teacher led	Independent Josh	Independent Kersten	Teacher led	Independent Tanya	Independent Jude
4: Tiffany Tim Nathan Matt Rosa Josh F.	Independent Tiffany	Independent Tim	Independent Nathan	Teacher led	Teacher led	Independent Matt	Independent Rosa	Independent Josh

Scholastic Professional Books, 1998

ing. Some of the questions students had written as well as some written by Carol were placed in a container that resembled a chocolate kiss. Students then took turns picking a question from the kiss. Using their books, students worked with their group to locate answers to the questions. Students signaled when their group found an answer and then read it aloud, giving the page and paragraph where they found the information. If correct, all the groups received a chocolate kiss. If incorrect, another group had the chance to respond. Play continued until all the questions were answered. This activity helped students like Matt learn how to reread for details. Those like Rosa benefited from meaningful practice.

Daily Routine for _The Chocolate Touch_

Whole Class (15 minutes)

- _Review happenings from the previous reading._
- _Introduce key vocabulary essential for comprehension._
- _Set purpose for reading._

Flexible Groups for Reading (30 minutes)

| Teacher Directed | Independent (student led) | Independent (student led) | Independent (student led) |

All Groups

- _Read chapter(s)._
- _Respond in literature logs._
- _Write question._
- _Discuss events._

Whole Class (15 minutes)

- _Share comments._
- _Revisit opening discussion._
- _Share questions._

TIP: If you want to try Carol's _Chocolate Touch_ lesson but have only five or six copies of the book, place students in groups to rotate through different language arts centers while you lead one group in guided reading. After each group has read the chapter with you, hold a class discussion. The floor plan (shown on page 63) shows one way to arrange a classroom for this kind of flexible grouping.

Pat's Grouping for Skill Instruction: 3 Days

To teach Jamie and the other children who needed help with word-by-word matching, Pat grouped them together during what she called free-choice time from 2:00 to 2:20. To organize for this period, Pat wrote each child's name on a tongue depressor. She then created a large pocket chart listing the activities from which the children could choose. She labeled one pocket "Teacher Group" and placed the name of children receiving skill instruc-

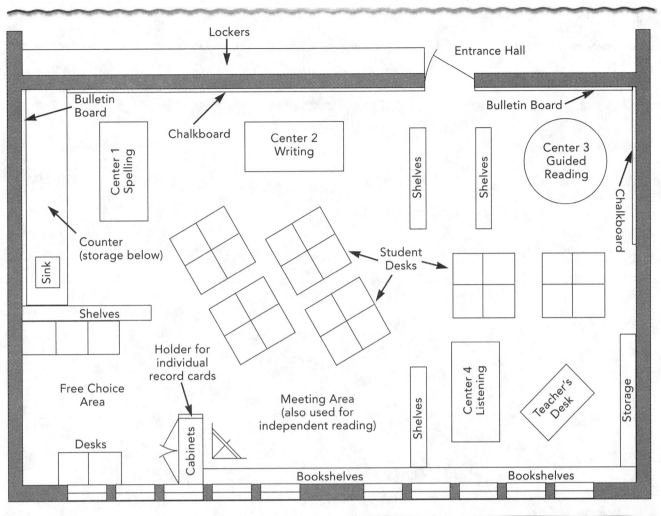

- Lockers
- Entrance Hall
- Bulletin Board
- Bulletin Board
- Chalkboard
- Center 1 Spelling
- Center 2 Writing
- Shelves
- Shelves
- Center 3 Guided Reading
- Counter (storage below)
- Sink
- Student Desks
- Chalkboard
- Shelves
- Holder for individual record cards
- Free Choice Area
- Cabinets
- Meeting Area (also used for independent reading)
- Shelves
- Center 4 Listening
- Teacher's Desk
- Storage
- Desks
- Bookshelves
- Bookshelves

tion in this pocket. At free-choice time, the other students selected their activities by placing the tongue depressors in the corresponding pockets.

Grouping children in this manner gave Pat the flexibility of keeping a group intact for as long as needed. For example, at the end of the third session, the children in Jamie's group showed that they could match word by word, so Pat dissolved the group. She then consulted her matrix (see page 54) to choose students for the next skill instruction group.

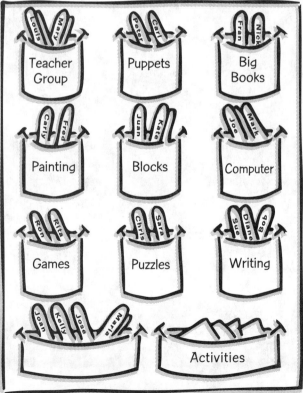

Teacher Group — Louis, Mary
Puppets — Peter, Carl
Big Books — Fran, Nick
Painting — Carly, Fred
Blocks — Juan, Kate
Computer — Joe, Mark
Games — Ron, Rita
Puzzles — Chris, Sara
Writing — Sue, Diane, Bob
Joan, Kelly, Jose, Maria
Activities

CHAPTER 4

Selecting Texts for Flexible Grouping

"If you want to make a reader, you have to find a book he can enjoy, one that makes him believe you think he can be a reader, and then you must help him find his way through it."

—New Zealand Department of Education

Teachers often ask me, "How do I pick material that is appropriate for all the different readers in my class?" The truth is, there may be times when you don't! In many situations, such as the one I described in the introduction to this book, teachers are given a "grade level" anthology to use.

Our solution was to use the anthology as a jumping-off place. We exposed children to the designated reader but selected additional trade books to help accomplish our many goals and objectives and to address the varying needs of our learners. Which takes us back to the opening question, "How do I pick material that is appropriate for all the different readers in my class?"

With so many children's books available, selecting books for flexible grouping can be a bit overwhelming. Fortunately, there are guidelines that can help you sort through the many books—guidelines I look at in this chapter. Clarifying some terms will help to provide the context for these guidelines.

WHAT IS GRADE LEVEL?

Grade-level books are those that children of a given age find appealing and interesting. The content is appropriate for children of a particular age and reflects child development characteristics. Complexity of the text is also deemed appropriate for a specific grade and is often determined by using a readability formula. This formula relies on sentence and word length to determine grade level. Oftentimes stories that meet these criteria are assembled in anthologies developed for specific grade levels. When children can read these books with ease or with minimal teacher guidance, they are said to be reading at grade level.

WHAT ARE READING LEVELS?

Reading levels are gauges of how well students can read given books. Each reader has three levels: easy, just right, and challenge. Research has established the commonly agreed upon criteria for each level.

Easy books are those that children can read with 96–100% word accuracy and 75–100% comprehension. At this level, children can identify nearly every word with ease and read fluently with much understanding. Because little guidance is needed with this type of book, it is often called the *independent level.*

Just-right books are those that children can read with 92–95% word accuracy and 60–75% comprehension. At this level, children need help with no more than one word in ten and read with good understanding. Because this is the level often used when teaching children new reading strategies or vocabulary, it is also called their *instructional level.*

Challenge books are those that children read with 90% or less word accuracy and 60% or less comprehension. At this level, children can identify few words and often have difficulty understanding the content. Books at this level require much support if the reading is to be somewhat successful. Because these books can be frustrating, this is often called the *frustrational level.*

My experience in working with many parents is that they often confuse these terms. Recognizing this, I developed this letter.

Scholastic Professional Books, 1998

Dear Family,

In a couple of weeks, I will be scheduling appointments with you to talk about your child's progress. I suspect that the one question I will hear most is, "Is my child reading on grade level?" Believe it or not, this is a complex question. You may well ask, "What's so hard about it? You're the teacher—don't you know?" These are good questions, and the purpose of this letter is to provide you with some answers.

Yes, I do know where your child is reading according to the materials I use to measure. However, children have three distinct reading levels—easy, just right, and challenge. The one I work with most—and the one you're undoubtedly most interested in when you inquire about grade level—is the just-right level. Let me explain.

Easy books are those that children can read with 96–100% word accuracy and 75–100% comprehension. At this level, children can identify nearly every word with ease and read fluently with much understanding. Because little guidance is needed with this type of book, it is often called the *independent level*.

Just-right books are those that children can read with 92–95% word accuracy and 60–75% comprehension. At this level, children need help with no more than one word in ten and read with good understanding. Because this is the level often used when teaching children new reading strategies or vocabulary, it is also called their *instructional level*.

Challenge books are those that children read with 90% or less word accuracy and with 60% or less comprehension. At this level, children can identify few words and often have difficulty understanding the content. Books at this level require much support if the reading is to be somewhat successful. This is often called the *frustrational level* because these books can be frustrating.

As you can see, the simple question has an involved answer! I think it's important for you to know how your child is performing. I believe that understanding these terms better provides you with this knowledge.

I'm looking forward to meeting you in the next couple of weeks.

Sincerely,
Michael F. Opitz

GUIDELINES FOR SELECTING BOOKS FOR FLEXIBLE GROUPING

1 **DETERMINE THE RANGE OF READING LEVELS WITHIN THE CLASS.** This will help you to select appropriate reading materials—easy, just right, and challenge—for your classroom library and specific groups. It will also help you to choose the appropriate teaching procedures, those that will lend the right amount of support for all students when they are reading texts of various levels. (Teaching procedures are discussed in Chapter 5 and Appendix 1.) To determine reading levels, use an informal reading inventory such as *Basic Reading Inventory* (Johns 1997), a running record, a set of graded passages, or benchmark books.

Here's what Brad, a fourth-grade teacher, did with his class.

Brad used a passage from a reading anthology to help him get a *general idea* of reading levels. He assessed each child individually as the others completed independent activities. He made notations on his copy of the passage and compiled the results on a class matrix. A *P* indicated that the child

---

Name _____ Brenda _____

Pettranella

Long ago in a country far away lived a little girl named Pettranella. She lived with her father and mother in the upstairs of her grandmother's tall, narrow house.

Other houses just like it lined the street on both sides, and at the end of the street was the mill. All day and all night smoke rose from its great smokestacks and lay like a grey blanket over the city. It hid the sun and choked the trees, and it withered the flowers that tried to grow in the window boxes.

One dark winter night when the wind blew cold from the east, Pettranella's father came home with a letter. The family gathered around the table in the warm yellow circle of the lamp to read it; even the grandmother came from her rooms downstairs to listen.

"It's from Uncle Gus in America," began her father. "He has his homestead there now, and is already clearing his land. Someday it will be a large farm growing many crops of grain." And then he read the letter aloud.

When he had finished, Pettranella said, "I wish we could go there, too, and live on a homestead."

Her parents looked at each other, their eyes twinkling with a secret. "We *are* going," said her mother. "We are sailing on the very next ship."

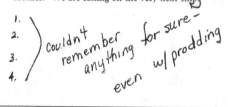

1.
2.
3.
4.
couldn't remember anything for sure— even w/ prodding

Teacher _____ Jenkins _____

Level 1 — Pettranella

Name	W. Rec. 0–12	Comp 3–4	P/F	Comments
Hank	10	+2	F	because of comp.
Meredith	4	+4	P	very fluent
Brenda	9	+0	F	looks like comp. needs work but could be expressive voc.
Jay	3	+3	P	fairly fluent; could retell a bit
Corey	3	+4	P	fluent
Kamal	1	+4	P	very fluent
Jason	26	+3	F	applies knowledge of phonics
Jack	4	+0	F	looks like comp. but most likely expression is what needs work
Holly	7	+2	F	very fluent; comp. appears weak
Marni	3	+4	P	very fluent
Sarah	3	+4	P	
Derrick	3	+4	P	
Ryan	1	+3	P	fluent
John	13	+2 1/2	P	—marginal
Sandi	0	+4	P	
Robyn	7	+4	P	fairly fluent
Annie	0	+4	P	
Kristy	1	+4	P	very fluent; good intonation
John	4	+4	P	very fluent
Jeff	0	+4	P	
Zack	21	+2 1/2	F	will need curr. adap. to read this text successfully
Jeff	11	+3	P	fairly fluent
Sara	0	+4	P	
Haitley	0	+3	P	
Tina	0	+4	P	
Kyle	1	+4	P	

Scholastic Professional Books, 1998

could read the passage at an instructional or independent level. An *F* indicated frustrational level. On this assessment, students had to attain 95% accuracy for a fourth-grade reading level. They were allowed up to 12 errors in word recognition (out of a 225-word passage) and had to retell the passage in their own words and answer questions about it.

2 **DETERMINE STUDENTS' INTERESTS.** Interest goes a long way in helping readers. In fact, research has shown that children can and do read well beyond their just-right level when they are reading books that are appealing to them. Interest, then, becomes an excellent way to hook them on reading. Just how can interests be identified? One way is by talking with students. You may also have students complete an inventory such as the one on page 31 telling about themselves and how they spend their free time. The Reading Interests profile at right shows how I used information from these inventories to create a class profile. This profile then guided my book selection and flexible reading groups. Note that Brenda's interests include animals.

Reading Interests Profile

Names \ Interests	animals	true stories	science fiction	fantasy	mysteries	stories about people	poetry	funny books	science topics	series books	magazines (sports)	magazines (computers)
Hank	✓									✓	✓	
Meredith			✓		✓							✓
Brenda	✓	✓					✓	✓				
Jay	✓		✓	✓		✓				✓		
Corey		✓				✓						
Kamal			✓						✓			
Jason	✓											
Joel					✓			✓				✓
Holly	✓		✓				✓	✓				
Marni	✓					✓					✓	
Sarah				✓			✓	✓				✓
Derrick		✓	✓	✓					✓			
Ryan												
John		✓				✓				✓		
Sandi										✓		
Robyn	✓									✓		
Annie		✓								✓		
Kurt				✓						✓		
Jeff												✓
Tina		✓	✓									
Hailey	✓											
Bo					✓			✓	✓		✓	
Jake		✓						✓			✓	
Shari								✓			✓	
Jessie	✓							✓		✓		

3 **CHOOSE BOOKS THAT YOU LIKE, TOO!** Teaching a book that we personally dislike rarely conveys feelings of pleasurable reading. Students pick up on our feelings and may, out of loyalty at the very least, decide that they don't like the book either. To be successful in modeling the pleasures of reading, then, we need to use books that we enjoy.

4 **CONSIDER READABILITY.** I think of readability as a willow branch that bends with the wind rather than a tree trunk that remains steady. The reason: Readability scores provide *estimates* of text difficulty rather than a definitive level. Why? Because the scores are determined by counting words in a sentence and syllables in words. Said another way, the formulas assume that the shorter the sentence and the fewer the syllables, the easier the book. However, research has shown that shorter, contrived sentences are often more difficult to read (Simons and Ammon 1989)! Also keep in mind that the formulas are not designed to assess what readers bring to the text—interest, background experiences, and knowledge of the topic at hand—variables that can facilitate successful reading. Even though Bill's instructional reading level was first grade, he was often able to read books far above this level when they were about one of his favorite topics—space. His interest carried him.

5 CONSIDER LANGUAGE FEATURES. Certain language patterns make reading easier. One example is rhyme; another is repetitive text. As the chart shows, these and other characteristics of natural language patterns are found in predictable books. Such books are excellent choices for children in kindergarten and first grade and for older struggling readers. Recognizing the benefits of predictable books, Pat provided her first grader Jamie with stories such as Eric Carle's *Have You Seen My Cat?*

PREDICTABLE BOOKS

Characteristic	Sample Title
supportive pictures	*Busy People* (Butterworth)
repeated sentence or phrase	*Just Like Daddy* (Asche)
rhyme and rhythm	*Time for Bed* (Fox)
cumulative pattern	*Jack's Garden* (Cole)
familiar cultural sequences	*Feast for 10* (Falwell)

TIP: The more of these characteristics a book has, the easier the story is to predict. Barbara Peterson offers a list of criteria to determine levels of predictability. See DeFord, Lyons, and Pinnell (119–147).

6 LOOK AT ILLUSTRATIONS AND FORMAT. A book's illustrations should be clear and should support the text. The format—the book's shape, print, layout, and design—should be inviting. Too many words or colors on a page can be distracting. To help children realize that they can read books of all sizes and shapes, choose a variety whenever possible. Include both hardbacks and paperbacks in your class library, as some students find the spacing in hardback versions easier to read. As Bill told me, "I like reading the hardback books because there's more room on the page."

7 THINK VARIETY. As you select books for your flexible groups, include a variety of genres. Each genre presents children with opportunities to read different types of texts, thereby making them stronger readers. Mysteries, poetry, informational books, fiction (realistic, science, and historical), biographies, and folklore are just some possibilities. Because Rosa tended to choose mostly nonfiction books about horses, Carol had her keep track of the kinds of books she read to see if she could read three different genres within a given period of time.

8 THINK MULTICULTURAL. The classroom collection should reflect our diverse society if we want to promote understanding of self and others. Using multicultural literature is one way to make children aware of other cultures. Of course, these books should be authentic and free of stereotypes. The following list, developed by the Notable Books for a Global Society Committee, shows evaluation criteria for selecting classroom books.

- Cultural accuracy

- Rich in cultural details

- Honor and celebrate diversity and common bonds

- In-depth treatment of cultural issues

- Characters within cultural group(s) interaction

- Purposeful inclusion of minority group members

- Invite reflection, critical analysis, and response

- Uniqueness in use of language or style

- Meets criteria for specific genre

- Appealing format; enduring quality

REFERENCES FOR SELECTING BOOKS

Books

More Books Kids Will Sit Still For by J. Freeman. Bowker, 1997.

Best Books for Children: Preschool Through the Middle Grades, ed. J. Gillespie and Christine Gilbert. Bowker, 1985.

Getting the Most from Predictable Books by M. Opitz. Scholastic, 1995.

Kaleidoscope: A Multicultural Booklist for Grades K–8 by R. Bishop. NCTE, 1994.

Just Right Books for Beginning Readers by Ellen Brooks Scholastic, 1996.

More Kids' Favorite Books. International Reading Association, 1985.

Raising a Reader by P. Kropp. Doubleday, 1996.

Through the Eyes of a Child by D. Norton. Merrill, 1987.

Periodicals

Booklinks. American Library Association.

The Dragon Lode. International Reading Association.

The Horn Book Magazine. Horn Book.

Interracial Books for Children. Council on Interracial Books for Children.

Language Arts. National Council Teachers of English.

The New Advocate. Christopher Gordon.

Parents' Choice: A Review of Children's Media. Parents' Choice Foundation

The Reading Teacher. International Reading Association.

9 **CONSIDER LITERARY ELEMENTS.** Look for books with worthy and appropriate themes, interesting plots, well-developed characters, and settings that enhance the plots.

10 **CHOOSE BOOKS THAT TIE INTO YOUR CURRICULUM AND THE FOCUS OF YOUR FLEXIBLE GROUPS.** Many books, both fiction and nonfiction, will tie into your curriculum. Others will help you integrate all content area instruction.

Try using the scale on page 73 as you select books for classroom use. You'll find many additional resources (see box) to help make this task easier. Also keep in mind that there are others who can assist you—for example, your students!

TEACHING CHILDREN TO CHOOSE THEIR OWN BOOKS

Teaching children how to select books is essential if we want to help them become lifelong readers. Choosing their own books is, after all, what they will do when they visit the library and/or bookstores outside of school.

Because book selection is a learned behavior, students may not always make what we consider to be the best choices. Some children also get "hooked" on one type of book—often one that is viewed as lacking the qualities of good literature. At times like these, a statement a colleague made to me several years ago may prove helpful: "Bad breath is better than no breath!" Children who work in flexible groups are exposed to variation in reading strategies and group membership. This flexibility, plus experience and guidance, helps students expand their horizons in reading; meanwhile, no matter what kind of books they select, they are still practicing their reading and getting better at it as a result.

On page 74 there are four ways that several teachers and I have used to help children choose worthwhile books.

> "When children are encouraged to share, discuss, and evaluate books, and given opportunities to do so, they are able to expand their reading enjoyment and to select worthwhile stories..."
>
> —D. Norton

Guideline Scale for Selecting Quality Books

SELECTIONS	low 1	2	3	4	high 5
Stories					
1. Is the plot original and believable?					
2. Are characters real and believable?					
3. Does the author avoid stereotyping?					
4. Is the theme of worth?					
5. Are style and language appropriate?					
6. Does the book have characteristics of a genre?					
7. How does it compare with others in same genre?					
Informational Books					
1. Does the book stimulate curiosity and wonder?					
2. Is the information accurate and current?					
3. Does the writer use facts to support ideas?					
4. Are stereotypes avoided?					
5. Is it clearly organized?					
6. Do illustrations help clarify information?					
7. Are there reference aids such as an index?					
Poetry					
1. Is it lively with exciting meters and rhythms?					
2. Does it emphasize sound of language?					
3. Does it encourage word play?					
4. Does the poem allow the reader to feel emotions?					
5. Will children want to hear it read more than once?					
6. Does the poem create images?					
7. Are poems arranged with enough space on the page?					

Scholastic Professional Books, 1998

Four Ways to Teach Book Selection

1 **HAVE CHILDREN GENERATE CRITERIA.** Involving students in determining the criteria helps them better understand what it is they need to look for. Post a list of their criteria and encourage the class to refer to the list when selecting books. Second-grade teacher Sarah Adams' students developed the following list for their classroom:

On the Easy Side
It's like you just run through the book.
Can read it fast.
Read it in two seconds.
You don't stumble over any words.
You don't have to skip words.
You enjoy it!
You finish quickly.
You know it like the back of your hand!
You get cramps in your mouth when you're reading it aloud.

Just Right
You stumble over some words, but the only way to get better is to figure them out.
A little slower but not too slow.
The story's exciting!
Some words you don't know but mostly you can figure them out.
You stop and look closely at some words but mostly you can figure them out.
You know the strategy to use.

On the Hard Side
You find a lot of words you don't know—It doesn't make sense!
Words get complicated.
Sometimes you have to sound out the words a lot.
Some words you don't understand.
You stumble over words.
You reread a lot.
The type of print may be too hard.
You feel frustrated.
You want to quit.
You have to stop a lot.
There are about 3 words you know and 20 you don't know!

FLEXIBLE GROUPING IN READING • SELECTING TEXTS FOR FLEXIBLE GROUPING
Scholastic Professional Books, 1998

2 **EXPLAIN TO STUDENTS HOW TO USE THE "THUMB" TEST.** This test has been around for quite a few years and has proven helpful for many students.

> 1. Open the book to the middle.
>
> 2. Open up your right or left hand.
>
> 3. Read a page of the book to yourself.
>
> 4. Put one finger down every time you come to a word you don't know.

If you finish the page and your thumb is still up, you probably have a book that is good for you.

3 **PROVIDE CHILDREN WITH A LIST OF QUESTIONS.** Use the list of questions on page 76 or devise a set of your own.

4 **READ ALOUD PARTS OF BOOKS.** By reading aloud to the class, you can help children to see that there are many good books aside from those they consider their favorites. By moving beyond the familiar, students read more types of books with a variety of text structures.

Name_____

Easy Books

Ask yourself these questions. If you circle YES, this book is probably an easy one for you.

1. Have you read it before?	YES	NO
2. Can you read it without stumbling?	YES	NO
3. Can you tell the ideas to someone else?	YES	NO

Just Right Books

Ask yourself these questions. If you circle YES, this book is probably just right for you.

1. Have you read it before?	YES	NO
2. Can you read most words?	YES	NO
3. Can you tell the ideas to someone else?	YES	NO
4. Could you read the book if you had a little help?	YES	NO

Challenge Books

Ask yourself these questions. If you circle NO to #1 & 2 and YES to #3 & 4, this book is probably going to be a little difficult for you.

1. Have you read it before?	YES	NO
2. Can you read most words?	YES	NO
3. Does the book confuse you?	YES	NO
4. Would you need lots of help to read it?	YES	NO

Adapted from M. Ohlauser and M. Jepsen, 1992.

FLEXIBLE GROUPING IN READING • SELECTING TEXTS FOR FLEXIBLE GROUPING

Scholastic Professional Books, 1998

CHAPTER 5

Planning for Successful Reading Experiences in Flexible Groups

"No single-faceted plan . . . will meet the requirements of every student. As we move toward alternative grouping plans, we must be careful to avoid the rigidity that characterizes traditional ability grouping and offer students dynamic and flexible opportunities responsive to curricular goals and individual needs."

—M. Radenrich, and L. McKay

You'd like to try flexible grouping but still have many unanswered questions. How can you plan lessons so that all children have access to good literature? What are some effective literature response strategies that you can build flexible groups around? This chapter presents suggestions to address questions such as these.

TWO IMPORTANT QUESTIONS FOR FLEXIBLE GROUPING

As with any teaching, you need a plan of action when using flexible grouping. To ensure that students gain the most from your reading program, first ask yourself these two important questions.

1 **WHAT ARE THE GOALS OF THE PROGRAM?** This question is critical because the goals provide the overall structure into which daily lessons fit. The goals listed below are those that several other teachers and I decided on when thinking about what we wanted for all students.

- To create readers who choose to read for a variety of purposes

- To have all children learn to read by doing a lot of reading

- To show students that there are skills/strategies common to all

- To show students that regardless of "level," all can read a given story and participate in a discussion

- To provide all children with opportunities to respond to literature in a variety of ways (e.g., talking, acting, writing, creating visual displays)

- To expose all children to the same "grade level" reading vocabulary

- To develop every child's reading and listening comprehension

2 **WHAT INSTRUCTIONAL FRAMEWORK WILL ENSURE THE SUCCESS OF ALL STUDENTS?** The three-phase instructional framework shown here (developed by Herber 1978) works well when using flexible grouping in a reading program.

Instructional Phase	Purpose
Before reading	Prepare students for the reading.
	1. Activate or build background knowledge.
	2. Arouse curiosity/build interest.
	3. Address any individual needs.
	4. Set purpose.
During reading	Provide time for students to read with or without teacher direction.
After reading	Provide an opportunity for students to respond to the reading; readers demonstrate understanding.

TEACHING STRATEGIES

There are many teaching strategies you can use for each phase. I list several here along with a brief description. (See Appendix A for more specific details. Yopp and Yopp 1996 provides additional ideas for each phase.)

TIP: When first introducing students to a new teaching strategy, use a familiar text so that you and the students can focus on the new strategy.

---

6 BEFORE-READING TEACHING STRATEGIES

Strategy	Brief Description
Anticipation guide	Students read statements before reading the text.
Brainstorming	Students state everything they know about a topic. All responses are accepted.
K-W-L	Students tell everything they think they know and want to know about a subject. Responses are written .
Literature response logs	Students write predictions or questions they want answered.
Previewing	Students read subheads and visuals before reading text.
Picture walk	Students look through all pictures in the story.

6 DURING-READING STRATEGIES

Strategy	Brief Description
Cut-apart	A story is cut into sections, one section for each class member. Each section is read in sequence.
Cooperative reading activity(CRA)	Students read a given section of text and come to an agreement on three important ideas to share with the rest of the class. Each group reads a different section.
Genre study	Students read stories that relate to a given genre.
Text set	Students read stories that relate to a topic. Stories correspond to instructional reading levels.
Single title, varied mode	All students read the same book but in different ways (e.g. ,teacher assist, partner, tape recorded).
Paired reading	Two students read together.

10 AFTER-READING TEACHING STRATEGIES

Strategy	Brief Description
• Class mural	Students create a mural showing the highlights or sequence of the story.
• Choral reading	Students read the story or part of the story aloud for the rest of the class.
• Comparison/contrast	A Venn diagram is used to show how characters or stories are alike and different.
• Drama	Students reenact all or a part of the story.
• K-W-L	Students write down what they learned in the learn column of the chart.
• Literature response logs	Students respond to the story through writing or drawing.
• Puppet theater	Students create puppets and use them to tell the story.
• Readers' theater	Students take the roles of story characters and read the story in play format.
• Retelling	Students retell everything they can recall about the story. This can be done orally or in writing.
• Sketch to stretch	Students sketch what the selection meant to them. Others tell what they think the sketch represents .

PLANNING GROUPS SO THAT ALL CHILDREN CAN SUCCEED

Given the numerous teaching strategies, the possibilities are endless! In fact, the many options may leave you feeling overwhelmed. Here are five steps to follow. You can use the blank lesson plan form on page 86 each step of the way.

1 DECIDE ON THE OBJECTIVE OF THE LESSON. What is it you want to accomplish with this particular lesson? Are you hoping to help students read more fluently? Is there a particular reading strategy you want students to learn? Do you want to expose all students to a specific type of genre?

2 CHOOSE THE TEXT(S) YOU WANT STUDENTS TO READ. As you may recall, one reason to use flexible grouping is to help all children read "grade level" texts. Therefore, at times you will want to have the entire class read the same text. Just *how* will all students be able to read the text(s)? The chart on page 81 shows how during-reading strategies provide support to diverse readers.

However, if children are to grow as readers, they also need to read material at their instructional levels. While exposing students to grade level texts with the necessary support is a good idea, at other times it is more appropriate for students to read at their instructional level.

Support provided by . . .	Cut-Apart	C R A	Genre Study	Text Set	Varied Mode	Paired Reading
enabling students to use repeated reading to develop reading fluency.	✔	✔		✔		
enabling students to practice reading before performing before the group.	✔	✔	✔	✔	✔	
establishing a meaningful context for oral reading.	✔	✔		✔		✔
giving students a manageable chunk of text to read.	✔	✔	✔	✔	✔	✔
expecting all students to read real books.	✔	✔	✔	✔	✔	✔
exposing students to several different genres and text structures, thereby expanding their ability to read a variety of texts for a variety of purposes.			✔	✔	✔	✔
permitting students to use their strongest modality to read a text.					✔	
teaching students how to glean important ideas from text.		✔	✔			
teaching students about story elements.			✔	✔	✔	✔
offering books related to an overall theme yet at different instructional reading levels.			✔	✔		
reading with students when necessary.	✔	✔	✔	✔	✔	
creating a nonthreatening atmosphere.	✔	✔	✔	✔	✔	✔
inviting peers to provide support for one another.		✔	✔	✔	✔	✔

3 *Think through grouping options.* As you have read, there are several ways to group students, and the use of flexible grouping assumes variety within a lesson. Students may be grouped for each phase—before, during, after—of a reading lesson with different grouping techniques used each time. Generally speaking, however, I like to begin and end a lesson with the whole class because it helps to build a sense of community, one of the reasons I use flexible grouping.

> "There is no single organizational scheme that we can simply put in place and leave alone."
> —R. Allington

For the second phase of the lesson, the during-reading part, I have found that different grouping options lend themselves to certain teaching strategies. The chart shows these connections. Besides using it to make decisions about the types of groups to use, you can use it to track how often you form each type of group. Why keep track? To make sure that you take advantage of the different grouping options.

CONNECTING GROUPING OPTIONS AND TEACHING STRATEGIES

Grouping Options	Cut-Apart	C R A	Varied Mode	Paired Reading	Genre Study	Text Set
random	✔	✔		✔		
achievement			✔		✔	✔
cooperative		✔	✔	✔	✔	✔
interest			✔	✔	✔	✔
task	✔		✔	✔		
knowledge				✔	✔	✔
skill/strategy	✔		✔			✔
student choice			✔	✔	✔	✔

Keep in mind that the literature will sometimes help you choose the best teaching strategy and grouping option. Consider the following four examples.

Example #1: You want to have students read Laura Numeroff's *Two For Stew*. A quick read of the book helps you to see that **pair reading** would be a good teaching strategy to use because the story is a conversation between a customer and a waiter. The parts are easy to depict because the book uses two different fonts—one for the customer and another for the waiter. But which grouping option will you use? Because you are primarily concerned with having groups equal in size, you use **random grouping.** You place an equal number of customer cards numbered 1 to 12 and waiter cards numbered the same way in a paper bag. You have each child take a card from the bag and pair up with the student holding the same number. That is, waiter #1 pairs with #1 customer.

Example #2: You want your whole class read Patricia Polacco's *In Enzo's Splendid Garden*. You recognize that the amount of text will overwhelm some readers in your class. You also recognize that the text is very repetitive and cumulative. In fact, it follows the pattern used in *The House That Jack Built* by Janet Stevens. As a result, you select the **cut apart** for your teaching strategy. You decide to use the **achievement grouping** option to ensure that all students will succeed. Therefore, you assign specific parts to certain children.

Example #3: You want all students to read Robert Snedden's *What Is a Bird?* This is a nonfiction book, and a quick glance reveals that you will need to provide some type of support for several readers. You decide to use the **cooperative reading activity** for your teaching strategy. Because the text appears in six chunks, you use **cooperative** grouping. Each group will read a different chunk and report the most essential information to the rest of the class.

Example #4: You want all students to read a common text such as Lois Lowry's *Number the Stars*. Recognizing that the text is too difficult for some students, you choose the **single title, varied mode** teaching strategy. This time you group children by **task** because it will enable them to read the text using their strongest modality.

4 **SELECT TEACHING STRATEGIES FOR EACH PHASE OF THE LESSON.** Refer to the chart on page 81 and Appendix A for an idea of the possible strategies to use to meet your objective. Keep in mind that you may use different strategies at different phases of a lesson.

5 **GATHER ALL NECESSARY MATERIALS.** Good teaching requires preparation. Checking to see that all materials are at hand makes success more likely.

CLASSROOM SCENARIO

Let's take a look at how Mary, a third grade teacher, and I used these steps to develop a lesson plan. Page 85 shows our complete two-day plan and the diagram on that page illustrates where we used flexible grouping in the lesson.

Choosing Objectives

As part of a larger unit on folktales, Mary and I chose three objectives: to develop students' reading fluency, to enhance their listening comprehension, and to teach them the characteristics of folktales.

Choosing the Text

For a text we chose *Bringing the Rain to Kapiti Plain* by Verna Aardema, one of the many folktales included in the newly adopted basal reading series we were expected to use with all third graders.

Grouping, Teaching Strategies, and Materials

Day 1

Before Reading Because we wanted to build community and to set the stage for successful reading by all students, we started with the whole class. We first used the folktale matrix (see below) to remind students of elements commonly found in folktales. Next, we told the students that the tale they would be reading would have some or all of these elements and that the tale was from Africa. After locating Africa on the map, we introduced the terms *Kapiti Plain, Ki-pat,* and *acacia.* Finally, we had students do a picture walk (see Appendix A for an explanation) through the book.

FOLK TALE MATRIX

Titles	Characteristics				
	Use of repetition	Characters with magical powers	Magical transformation occurs	Magic object used	Trickery used

During Reading We decided to use the **cut-apart** as a teaching strategy because we wanted to focus on building students' fluency and listening comprehension. In this strategy, each student practices reading a numbered section of a text and then joins the rest of the group to read aloud the whole story. We also recognized that the book had several supportive language features such as repetition and cumulative text, which would help less fluent readers like Brenda.

We prepared the necessary materials and explained the procedure to the class. I also printed the entire story on chart paper, using different colors for each new verse and black for repeated verses. As students practiced reading their part of the story silently, Mary and I walked around the room, assisting those who signaled us for help.

When students finished practicing, we had them sit in a circle on the floor in numerical order. Each student then read his or her part in turn while the others listened.

FLEXIBLE GROUPING IN READING • PLANNING FOR SUCCESSFUL READING EXPERIENCES
Scholastic Professional Books, 1998

Day 2

We began by **randomly** grouping students in sets of four. We gave each group one page of the chart paper version of the story to practice reading. This provided students with a chance to read parts of the folktale that they may not have read while using the **cut apart** strategy. All the chart pages were then put on display.

After Reading Using the charts, each group read aloud its part in turn. The whole class joined in to read the words in black print. Students could clearly see how the text was cumulative—the amount of text on each chart page increased as the story progressed. To emphasize a sense of community, we had students create a class mural. Each group drew illustrations that coincided with its part of the story. We covered a large portion of a wall with chart paper and had students re-create *Bringing the Rain to Kapiti Plain* by affixing their illustrations as they orally reread their part of the story once more.

Together, then, all three phases—before, during, and after reading—provide a thorough lesson that helps students become stronger readers. Readers such as Brenda become stronger because through flexible grouping they are exposed to a grade level text and taught how to read and respond to it. Fluent readers become stronger by reading yet another piece of quality literature and responding to it.

FLEXIBLE GROUPING LESSON PLAN

Objective: _to build fluency; to enhance listening comprehension_

Selection (s): _Bringing the Rain to Kapiti Plain_

Considerations	Teaching Procedures
Before	1. Remind students about common folktale elements by referring to the grid.
Grouping Technique: whole group	2. Tell students that the folktale they will be reading today may have some or all of these elements and is a Nandi Tale (from Africa).
Teaching Strategy: • picture walk • folktale grid	3. Invite students to find Bringing the rain to Kapiti Plain in the Table of Contents, turn to it, and do a picture read (look at pictures only). Invite predictions.
Materials: • books	4. Introduce vocabulary: Kapiti Plain, Ki-Pat, and acacia using sentences from the story.
During	1. Explain the Cut-Apart procedure (see p. 00).
Grouping Technique: ✔ whole group ✔ individual ✔ small groups of _4_ each	2. Allow students time to practice reading silently. Assist those who need extra help with their sections.
Assignment by: ✔ random ___ task ___ achievement ___ interest ___ knowledge ___ social ___ skill/strategy ___ student choice	3. Have students sit in a circle in numerical order. 4. Have each read his/her part in turn. 5. Collect cards. 6. Display posters.
Teaching Strategy: Cut-apart Choral rereading	7. Randomly assign students to groups and give each group a poster written with a different color. 8. allow time for groups to practice reading.
Materials: • Cards (one for ea. student)	9. Explain procedure for reading posters in turn and reading block print. 10. Display posters in order and do the choral reading.
After	1. Tell each group that they need to illustrate their part of the story using art supplies on the back counter.
Grouping Technique: ___ whole group ___ individual ✔ small groups of _4_ each	2. Tell students that their illustrations will enable us to have our own Kapiti Plain.
Assignment by: ✔ random ___ task ___ achievement ___ interest ___ knowledge ___ social ___ skill/strategy ___ student choice	3. Provide students time to create. 4. Have groups add their illustration to the Plain in turn, reading their part as they do so.
Teaching Strategy: • Class mural • Choral reread	
Materials: • posters showing story • art supplies	

Bringing the Rain to Kapiti Plain Lesson

Whole Class
Before Reading

- Talk about elements of folktales—refer to grid.
- Provide background about today's story.
- Invite students to preview.
- Introduce key vocabulary.

Flexible Grouping
During Reading

- Individual reading practice
- Group reading practice

Whole Class
After Reading

- Groups illustrate.
- Entire class does choral reading.

FLEXIBLE GROUPING LESSON PLAN

Objective: _____

Selection (s): _____

Considerations	Teaching Procedures
Before	
Grouping Technique:	
Teaching Strategy:	
Materials:	
During	
Grouping Technique: ___ whole group ___ individual ___ small groups of ___each	
Assignment by: ___ random ___ task ___ achievement ___ interest ___ knowledge ___ social ___ skill/strategy ___ student choice	
Teaching strategy:	
Materials:	
After	
Grouping Technique: ___ whole group ___ individual ___ small groups of ___each	
Assignment by: ___ random ___ task ___ achievement ___ interest ___ knowledge ___ social ___ skill/strategy ___ student choice	
Teaching Strategy:	
Materials:	

FLEXIBLE GROUPING IN READING • PLANNING FOR SUCCESSFUL READING EXPERIENCES

Scholastic Professional Books, 1998

CHAPTER 6

Checking Progress in Flexible Grouping

"In our day to day teaching, we must constantly test and revise our initial judgments, modify our strategies, and recreate our estimates."

—J. Gillet and C. Temple

Flexible grouping accommodates not only the differences in young readers but also the changes that they undergo throughout the school year. Students' growth as readers necessitates constant monitoring. This chapter focuses on some practical ways to assess individual children—even while the rest of the class is present. You'll also find some ideas for easy record keeping.

ASSESSING INDIVIDUALS WITHIN A FLEXIBLE GROUPING FRAMEWORK

Here are four practical ways to assess children within a flexible grouping framework.

1 **STUDENT PRODUCTS.** One way of checking progress is to look at what students produce. Their work not only shows that they have completed an activity but also their level of understanding. For example, Bill, the third grader who had a first-grade instructional level, completed the story map for *Big Max* (see Chapter 1), independently showing his ability to identify pertinent information.

2 **STUDENT COMMENTS.** Talking with students can reveal their views of where they see themselves. It never ceases to amaze me just how on target kids can be! For example, after Bill read a page of a story to me—a page that proved difficult from my calculated view—I asked him what he thought:

Me: So what do you think, Bill? Was this too easy, just right, or a challenge?

Bill: Kind of too hard.

"Don't talk that way," said Anna. "This is not funny! I've had enough sausages. What can we do to get out of this?"

"Well," said Fritz, "your wish is gone and mine is gone. But together we have one wish left. Let's WISH to get out from under the sausages."

3 **ONGOING USE OF ASSESSMENT TECHNIQUES.** Some of the strategies discussed in Chapter 2 provide opportunities for ongoing assessment. For example, Jamie, the first grader who needed to learn print concepts, demonstrated her growth by reading *Poor Old Polly* by June Melser and Joy Cowley to me during independent reading time. As she read, I took a running record. An analysis revealed that she had learned word matching and that she was using some effective reading strategies: decoding, repeating to correct herself, and visual cues when making substitutions.

4 **INTEGRATING ASSESSMENT WITH UNITS OF STUDY.** Viewing assessment as an integral part of units of study rather than as an event that happens two or three times a year helps to validate learning with greater accura-

cy. Take, for example, what occurred with Brenda when Mary and I were conducting our folktale unit. I made a copy of the story Brenda was reading. While she and the others were reading independently, I sat down next to her and asked her to read me page 7. The markings on page 88 show how Brenda performed. From this brief measure, I could see that Brenda's phrasing was improving, that she was starting to monitor her reading as evidenced by the way she self corrected, and that she was beginning to make some meaningful substitutions. She was also using words that looked similar to those in the text.

KEEPING TRACK OF STUDENT PROGRESS

There are many ways to track students' growth, many ways of identifying "glimmers of success." Here are three.

1 **INVOLVE STUDENTS.** Begin by converting the "I" to "we"! Yes, students can and should be part of the process. This involvement helps children to see their own growth and to feel responsible for their learning. Students can help by . . .

- *Keeping their own reading logs.* The form on page 28 in Chapter 2 shows one possibility.

- *Keeping track of the types of books they read.* Textflips such as the one illustrated here are a handy way to accomplish this task. Students fill in a circle to indicate the type of book they've just read. Then they flip open the door and write the title, author, and illustrator on the first blank page. On the back of that page, they write how well they liked the book and how difficult they found it to be (easy, just right, or challenge). After students have filled in three circles for one kind of genre, they move on to other types of books. The idea is to read an equal number of books in different genres.

- *Filing their own papers.* Not only does it save you time, it also provides a meaningful lesson in alphabetizing. If you are using portfolios, have students maintain them.

TIP: *Portfolios in the Classroom* (Scholastic, 1994) is an invaluable resource for showing effective use of portfolios. Coauthored by five teachers, it offers specific ideas for organizing the process right from the beginning of the year.

---

2 **KEEP ANECDOTALS.** "I've decided to start this notebook which I'm going to call *glimmers of success*. What I'm going to do is write down any episodes that let me know that our flexible grouping ideas are helping all of our students to be better readers." And so my "glimmers" journal was born.

Indeed, keeping anecdotal records is one way of documenting student progress. Consider these three examples.

Monday, November 20
When previewing a story the whole class was going to read, Bill volunteered to read a caption for one of the pictures. He needed my support to read some of the words, but he didn't appear to be bothered by this. Later, in his cooperative group, I saw him reading his important information to the other students. I'm thrilled that he was willing to take these risks. Can this be the same child who, in September, told me that he couldn't do the assignment because he was "special ed"?

Tuesday, November 21
Jamie participated with the rest of the class as they chorally read their turkey book. She then read it by herself, pointing to each word as she read. She really is showing that she has developed "wordness"! I am convinced that the skill group she was part of helped her to acquire this most important skill.

Wednesday, December 10
I'm getting better at managing conferences. Keeping them short and focused has helped a lot. I also like my idea of focusing on five children each day, as this is so much easier to manage. I give each set of five the same color tab in my anecdotal records notebook—that is a good reminder to concentrate on those children that day. This rotation has enabled me to meet with every child at least once a week.

2 **USE RECORD-KEEPING FORMS THAT YOU FULLY UNDERSTAND!** There are several commercially prepared checklists that provide the illusion of being ready to go and saving you time. However, most of these will save you time only if you read through them to make sure you fully understand every item listed. If you don't understand a form, change it by rewording or deleting. The form on page 91 was created by doing just that!

- -

TIP: The best system is one that reflects you and your way of organizing. Don't be afraid to set up your own method for informal assessment of student progress.

- -

Scholastic Professional Books, 1998

Name _____ Date _____

LITERACY DEVELOPMENT CHECKLIST

	does not apply	most of the time	sometimes	not noticed yet
1. Interest in Books				
is willing to read				
shows pleasure in reading				
selects books independently				
chooses books of appropriate difficulty				
samples a variety of genres				
2. Book Knowledge				
identifies title, author, and illustrator				
3. Reading Strategies				
uses knowledge of language to understand text				
uses meaning clues in context				
uses meaning clues from prior experience				
uses sentence structure clues				
substitutes a word with similar meaning				
sounds out				
uses rhyme and pattern				
uses word structure clues				
uses story structure clues				
views self as reader				
notices miscues if they interfere with meaning				
infers words in close-type activities				
takes risks as a reader (guesses)				
summarizes major events in a story				
remembers sequence of events				
demonstrates predicting and confirming				
attends to reading independently				

Scholastic Professional Books, 1998

CHAPTER 7

Looking at the Whole Program

"A literature program should help students enjoy books, recognize and appreciate good literature, understand their heritage, and understand themselves and others."

—D. Norton

An effective, balanced reading program is made up of several components. In this chapter I take a look at these to put flexible grouping in proper perspective. Sample schedules show how some teachers fit each of these components into their school day. The chapter concludes with a few reminders for you—and parents, too!

FLEXIBLE GROUPING IN THE TOTAL READING PROGRAM

Flexible grouping can take place throughout the school day to facilitate learning. As it relates to reading instruction and as it is discussed in this book, however, flexible grouping occurs when the teacher is providing much support to help students read. This is often called guided reading, because the teacher is doing just that, guiding the reading.

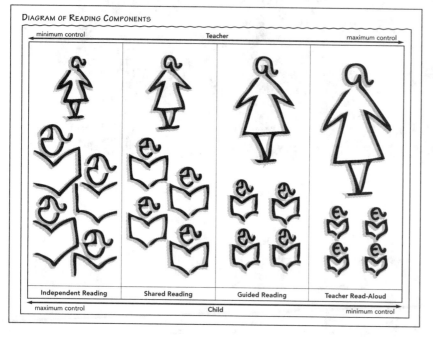

DIAGRAM OF READING COMPONENTS

minimum control — Teacher — maximum control

Independent Reading — Shared Reading — Guided Reading — Teacher Read-Aloud

maximum control — Child — minimum control

Guided reading provides a meaningful context to teach specific reading skills and strategies. Guided reading also provides an opportunity for literature discussion groups. Sometimes these groups are led by students while the teacher circulates to provide guidance. At other times, the teacher guides the discussion.

Guided reading is but one component of a balanced reading program. Other essential components are *independent reading, shared reading,* and *teacher read aloud.*

The chart above shows how teacher and student control ebbs and flows in the course of the total reading program. The pie charts on page 96 show how the components fit together to create a balanced reading program in the primary and intermediate grades. The chart on page 95 describes these components. These graphics illustrate that all children must be afforded many opportunities to read at school if they are to become readers. Remember, too, that children need a balance of reading materials—those that enable them to achieve success with ease as well as those that challenge, if they are to continue to grow in their ability to read more complex material (Berliner 1981).

NOTE: Although the focus of this book is on the use of flexible grouping in reading, writing is also part of an effective reading program. Writing demands much critical thinking. The writer must organize ideas and use words to express thoughts to create a text for others to read. Other times, the writer uses words to show understanding of a text—to respond to reading for oneself or an audience. It is also a meaningful way for a learner to apply what he or she knows about letters, sounds, words, and other print conventions. As with reading, the teacher needs to provide more or less

Scholastic Professional Books, 1998

COMPONENTS OF A BALANCED READING PROGRAM

Component	Purposes	What Student Does	What Teacher Does	Approx. Time
Independent Reading Students choose their own texts to read alone with a partner, or with a group.	• to experience the joys of reading • to enable all students to learn to read by reading • to provide all students with self-selection of books • to provide meaningful practice • to provide a sense of community	• Chooses texts • Reads on own with a friend or a group, either silently or orally	• Models reading by reading own book • Talks with students about texts • At times, captures "teachable moment" and teaches a given skill or strategy • Assesses reading fluency with individual students	10-30 minutes
Guided Reading Teacher directs all students through the reading of a text using flexible grouping strategies. Students sometimes guide discussion groups while teacher facilitates.	• to show students the joys of reading • to provide instruction at an appropriate level • to provide meaningful contexts for instruction of word analysis, vocabulary, and comprehension • to facilitate all students' reading growth by expecting all to read connected text	• Reads text and applies known strategies • Participates in discussions • Responds to literature in some manner	• Plans lesson that will enable successful reading for all learners • Instructs students • Assesses reading behaviors	60 minutes
Shared Reading Teacher reads a book and invites children to join in.	• to show students the joy of reading • to demonstrate reading strategies • to provide for individual differences without labels	• Listens • Joins in reading if shared reading; responds to inquiries if doing interactive reading • Talks about the reading	• Reads orally • Invites students to join in • At times, may point out features of text • May ask students to point to words using a pointer • Assess students	30 minutes
Teacher Read-Aloud Teacher or children choose a book for the teacher to read to the whole group.	• to show students the joy of reading • to develop a sense of community • to model fluent, purposeful oral reading • to expose children to various forms of literature	• Listens • Responds to pictures or text	• Reads orally • May stop to answer questions or develop suspense	15–20 minutes

Scholastic Professional Books, 1998

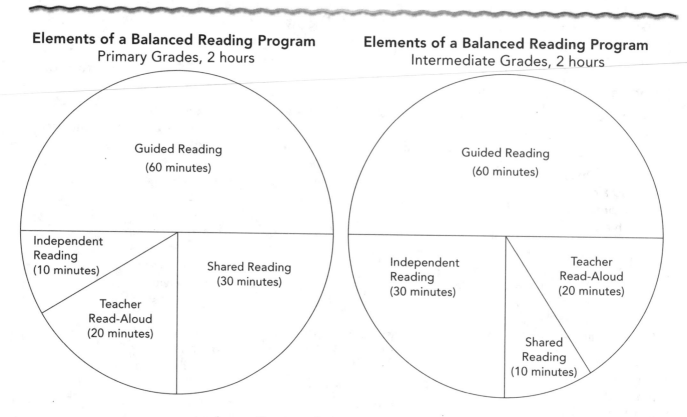

Elements of a Balanced Reading Program
Primary Grades, 2 hours

- Guided Reading (60 minutes)
- Independent Reading (10 minutes)
- Teacher Read-Aloud (20 minutes)
- Shared Reading (30 minutes)

Elements of a Balanced Reading Program
Intermediate Grades, 2 hours

- Guided Reading (60 minutes)
- Independent Reading (30 minutes)
- Teacher Read-Aloud (20 minutes)
- Shared Reading (10 minutes)

support depending on the purpose for the instruction. Different writing lessons require the student to function at different levels of independence.

TIP: For ideas on ways to teach writing and ways to integrate writing with reading, three resources I have found to be invaluable are: L. Calkins, *The Art of Teaching Writing*, D. Graves, *A Fresh Look at Writing*, and L. Bridges, *Writing as a Way of Knowing*.

SOME SAMPLE SCHEDULES

Just how all of the components of a total reading program fit into a day varies from teacher to teacher. Here are four samples.

Schedule #1: Lou Grimes's First Grade

8:00–8:10:	Settling-in time
8:10–8:25:	Interactive writing
8:25–8:50:	Journal and independent writing
8:50–9:00:	Shared reading
9:00–10:00:	Language arts centers (guided reading, listening, language study). **Flexible Grouping** occurs here. Centers may or may not be used.
10:00–10:15:	Teacher read-aloud
10:15–10:30:	Recess

10:30–11:00:	Mathematics
11:00–11:30:	Lunch (students also share books they have read at home)
11:30–12:00:	Word building
12:00–12:30:	Recess
12:30–12:55:	Independent reading
1:00–2:00:	Social studies, science, or art
2:00–2:05:	Review and dismissal

Lou extends the reading her students do through an at home reading program designed to encourage parent-child interactions with books and to instill a lifelong love of reading. Each student has a laminated manila envelope to transport books to and from school. Students check out the books from the classroom. Lou also encourages families to make use of books from other sources—book club purchases, the public library, borrowed books, newspapers, poems, songs, signs, labels, recipes, magazines— anything!

When a child can read a story with ease and fluency, the parent signs off and dates a form on which the book is recorded. This form is usually in a shape that relates to a theme students are studying. For example, the form might be an animal shape if the class is working on a nature study. Students bring the signed forms to school and tally the total number of books they have read as a class each day.

Schedule #2: Barbara Van Geystel's Second Grade

8:05–8:15:	Opening
8:20–9:45:	Language arts block (guided reading, writing, spelling). **Flexible grouping** used here.
9:45–10:00:	Morning recess
10:00–10:35:	Mathematics
10:35–10:55:	Specials (P.E., music, etc.)
11:00–11:25:	Lunch
11:30–11:55:	Teacher read-aloud
12:00–12:30:	Science/social studies
12:35–12:55:	Afternoon recess
1:00–1:25:	Independent reading
1:30–1:50:	Shared reading
1:50–2:00:	Dismissal

Scholastic Professional Books, 1998

Schedule #3: Brook Coleman's Fifth Grade

8:10–8:45:	Word study (etymology, proofreading, word structure)
9:00–9:45:	Mathematics
9:45–10:00:	Recess
10:00–11:00:	Reading. **Flexible grouping** is used here.
11:00–11:30:	Writing
11:35–12:00:	Lunch
12:00–12:30:	Independent reading. Parent volunteers (3 each week) come into the room at this time and read with students for ten minutes. All students read to a parent at least once a week. Students are allowed to pair up if they choose.
12:30–12:50:	Recess
12:55–1:15:	Teacher read-aloud
1:15–1:45:	Social studies. **Flexible grouping** is used here.
1:45–2:20:	Science/health/art
2:20–2:30:	Dismissal

Schedule # 4: Generic Schedule

8:00–8:15:	Opening
8:15–8:45:	Shared reading
8:45–9:45:	Guided Reading. Specific **flexible grouping** strategies used here.
9:45–10:00:	Recess
10:00–11:00:	Writing workshop
11:00–11:25:	Independent reading
11:30–12:30:	Lunch/recess
12:30–12:50:	Teacher read-aloud
12:50–1:35:	Mathematics
1:35–2:00:	Specials
2:00–2:10:	Afternoon recess
2:10–2:50:	Science/social studies
2:50–3:00:	Closing
3:00–3:15:	Dismissal

NOTE: Although this schedule shows designated times for given subjects, the schedule lends itself well to thematic studies. Large chunks of time and a self-contained classroom allow for much flexibility throughout the day.

FLEXIBLE GROUPING IN READING • LOOKING AT THE WHOLE PROGRAM
Scholastic Professional Books, 1998

A FEW REMINDERS FOR YOU— AND PARENTS TOO!

EVERY STUDENT MAY NOT READ OR UNDERSTAND EVERY SINGLE WORD OF EVERY TEXT SELECTION.
Remember that you are not always teaching for mastery. What you are attempting to do when using flexible grouping is expose all students to the same grade-level content. You are also providing the opportunity for *all* students to learn to read by reading with necessary support from others. In a sense, you are teaching the reader rather than the reading. That is, you are teaching all students how to read different texts and what to do when they encounter difficulties. You are also making sure that all students continue to develop their reading potential. To accomplish all this, you need *a variety of strategies and a variety of texts.*

> "When we limit reading material because we feel some students can't handle it, we limit the whole child, his or her relationships, and his or her personal view. We actually teach children to limit themselves."
> —N. Zaragota

ALL STUDENTS NEED OPPORTUNITIES TO READ "JUST RIGHT" MATERIAL OF THEIR CHOOSING AS A PART OF THE TOTAL READING PROGRAM.
This just-right material is essential for students to succeed in reading. In fact, students gain in reading achievement, vocabulary growth, and fluency as a result of reading this type of material during independent reading time (Anderson et al 1985).

TIP: Ellen Brooks's *Just-Right Books for Beginning Readers* (Scholastic, 1996) is one helpful resource. It provides an annotated bibliography of books along with suggested levels. I have also written a book called *Getting the Most from Predictable Books* . Other resources can be found in Chapter 4.

YOU MIGHT HAVE TO ALTER YOUR VIEW OF WHAT IT MEANS TO HAVE STUDENTS READ A TEXT.
If you believe that reading is reading every word on every single page, you need to rethink this definition when using several of the procedures presented in this book. I have discovered that there are many alternative ways that can help all students become stronger readers, those who can and do read real books for specific purposes.

As you have read, struggling readers are often afforded few opportunities to read books. Instead, they are in a corner of the room learning *about reading* while the rest of the class is learning to read *by reading*. However, the strategies described in this book enable such children to read books, too. Through this reading, they continue to learn new words and expand their knowledge base. I cannot emphasize enough the benefits of using a variety of grouping options and teaching procedures and exposing children to different types of reading experiences.

THE STUDENT WHO FINDS THE TEXT TOO EASY IS ALSO GETTING SOMETHING OUT OF THE EXPERIENCE EVEN THOUGH THIS READER MAY NOT HAVE LEARNED ANY NEW WORDS.

Why? Because reading is an active process—readers bring meaning to a page to get meaning from it. Therefore, because the reader interacts with the author's intended message to construct his or her own, much thinking has occurred.

TIP: A good example to use with parents to explain this point is one that they have undoubtedly experienced—that of reading the same book as a friend but constructing different ideas about it based on experience and background.

COMMUNICATE WITH FAMILIES.

My experience has been that many parents believe they have a good idea about what should be happening in school. They were, after all, students at one time. Flexible grouping may be new to them. Explaining it will help them to better understand what it is and why you are using it. What parents need to see is that flexible grouping is a way of ensuring that high expectations are established for all learners rather than watering down the curriculum. The sample letter on page 101 might be of help.

To further your communication with parents, you might want them to evaluate you. The evaluation form on page 102 is one that I have found useful.

TIP: I have found Bernice Cullinan's *Read to Me: Raising Kids Who Love to Read* an excellent resource for parents. It provides suggestions for how to read with their children along with some titles to try. It also provides a list of reading stages, descriptors of each, and ideas for working with children at each stage. Chapter nine and the appendixes of J. Johns and S. Lenski's *Improving Reading: A Handbook of Strategies* also provide a wealth of ideas for connecting home and school.

ENJOY TEACHING YOUR STUDENTS!

I often hear people talk about how teachers influenced their lives. How important, then, to let students know that we enjoy being with them and that we believe in them. Also keep in mind that not only do we influence our students—they influence us! They remain with us long after the school year ends.

Dear Family,

Welcome to _____ grade! I am thrilled to be teaching your child this year!

The beginning of a new school year is always exciting for me because I get another chance to teach to my best ability using what I have learned over the years.

If you are like other parents—myself included—you are probably wondering how reading will be taught. The main purpose of this letter is to answer this question.

My overall goal in teaching reading is to help your child learn to read at grade level and to instill a real desire to read—both in and out of school. I want him or her to see that reading is a pleasurable activity that is worth pursuing outside of school for fun as well as to acquire knowledge. Clearly, I have high expectations for every single learner.

To accomplish my goal, I group students in many different ways rather than placing them in one reading group for most of the year. This is often called flexible grouping. For example, sometimes I teach the entire class. Other times I group together children who need to learn specific skills. Still other times I have students read together in teams. There are also times when I group children according to like interests, as interest is a great motivator for reading. There are even times when I expect students to choose their own books and groups, as these choices help them feel more involved in their learning. Rest assured, however, that all of these grouping arrangements are done under my guidance, and all are designed to help me teach your child specific objectives of the reading program.

I firmly believe that using flexible grouping will be as successful this year as it has been in the past. It will enable me to make better use of my time as I go about providing for individual differences. I will also be better equipped to provide necessary support to your child when he or she is reading many kinds of books. Finally, it will help me provide opportunities for children to read with several different classmates over the year. Doing so will ensure that all come to better understand one another and see that all of us can contribute to one another's learning.

While this letter gives you the essence of the way I teach reading, you may want to come into our classroom to see what happens. I welcome your visits!

Thank you for the opportunity to know and teach your child. I am looking forward to a year filled with learning.

Sincerely,

Michael F. Opitz

Name_____

TEACHER EVALUATION

	Never	Rarely	Sometimes	Almost Always	Always
1. Have I:					
communicated with you effectively?					
shown respect to your child-rearing practices used at home?					
cooperated with you concerning your child's needs?					
made you feel that we are working together for the benefit of your child?					
made you feel welcome at any time?					
2. Do you feel that your child has:					
enjoyed school this year?					
improved in reading?					
improved in his or her ability to spell?					
learned to express himself or herself through writing?					
improved in mathematics?					
benefitted from my teaching style?					
grown emotionally and socially?					
learned to be responsible?					
the ability to make choices?					
learned to respect the rights of others?					
learned to cooperate and be considerate of others?					
learned to like himself or herself?					

3. Questions and Answers for More Insight

What do you feel is my biggest strength? Please explain.

_____

_____

_____

FLEXIBLE GROUPING IN READING • LOOKING AT THE WHOLE PROGRAM
Scholastic Professional Books, 1998

TEACHER EVALUATION

What do you feel is my biggest weakness? Explain.

_____

_____

_____

_____

What aspect does your child discuss most about his or her classroom experience?

_____

_____

_____

_____

4. Please feel free to add any comments regarding any aspect(s) on this evaluation.

_____

_____

_____

_____

_____

_____

Thank you very much for taking the time to complete and return this evaluation. Your honest replies will aid me in becoming a more effective educator.

With sincere thanks,

How-to Explanations of Reading Strategies in Flexible Grouping

Strategy	Before	During	After
Anticipation Guide	✔		
Brainstorming	✔		
K- W- L	✔	✔	✔
Literature Response Logs	✔	✔	✔
Previewing	✔		
Picture Walk	✔		
Cut Apart		✔	
Cooperative Reading Activity		✔	
Genre Study		✔	
Text Set		✔	
Single-Text, Varied Mode		✔	
Paired Reading		✔	
Class Mural			✔
Choral Reading			✔
Comparison/Contrast			✔
Drama			✔
Puppet Theater			✔
Readers Theater			✔
Retelling			✔
Sketch to Stretch			✔

TEACHING STRATEGIES FOR BEFORE READING

Here are descriptions for six activities to use during the first phase of a lesson,—the before-reading phase. Remember that the purpose of this part of the lesson is to activate or build background knowledge. It also enables you to arouse curiosity, build interest, address individual needs, and set a purpose for the reading. You may also want to introduce key vocabulary—words that students must understand in order to comprehend the material—at this time.

Taking time with this part of the lesson makes comprehension for all children more likely. Why? Because not all children automatically integrate what they know with what they are about to read; they have to be explicitly taught how to do so. Of course, our ultimate goal is to help learners internalize the strategies so that they will provide themselves with a warm-up on their own.

The following activities are of value for all learners, as they provide opportunities to discuss ideas and share knowledge. There are many reasons why a child may have difficulty reading. We cannot always assume that the struggling reader has nothing to contribute and that the fluent reader knows all there is to know about each and every topic. Deliberately planning lessons that make use of these strategies, then, gives students a chance to learn from one another. The activities can also serve as confidence boosters, especially for the child who has difficulty reading yet knows much about the topic.

Anticipation Guide (Readence, Bean, and Baldwin 1989)

Anticipation guides may vary in form, but all follow the same basic procedure:

1. The teacher reads the text and identifies the major concepts.

2. The major concepts are written as sentences.

3. Students read the statements and indicate whether they agree or disagree with each.

4. Students discuss their responses before reading the text.

5. Students read the text.

6. After reading, students revisit the guides and compare opinions during a discussion.

- -

TIP: A less formal and time-consuming variation of this guide calls for writing two or three statements on the board. Students receive the same number of Post-its as there are sentences. Each students writes yes or no on a Post-it and places it on the board next to the statement. Steps 5 and 6 are then followed.

- -

<u>Example</u>: Anticipation Guide for *Stories Julian Tells* by Ann Cameron

Agree	Disagree	Statement
_____	_____	1. All people tell stories.
_____	_____	2. Being the youngest in the family is fun.
_____	_____	3. Being an older brother is hard work.

Brainstorming

1. Students state everything they know about a topic within a certain time frame.

2. Write their responses on the board. To help show relationships among their statements, create a semantic map with the topic in the center.

3. Students begin reading.

K-W-L (Ogle 1986)

The first two steps of this teaching strategy lend themselves well to the before reading phase.

K (Know): Students tell you everything they think they know about the story they are about to read. Write students' ideas in the K column of a chart. Next, take their ideas and group them into any categories.

W (Want): Students tell you what they want to learn. Write their suggestions in the W column.

L (Learn): After students have finished reading, list what they learned in the L column of the K-W-L chart. They can also check the W column to see which questions were answered and which left unanswered and then revisit the K column to see if they had any misconceptions.

Literature Response Logs

Literature logs work for all three phases of a reading lesson. Here are some ways to use them before reading.

1. Students write one question they would like to have answered. They write the answer to their question when they are finished reading.

2. Students draw a picture of what they think might happen based on the title.

3. Students write their predictions. They then read and note where their prediction was validated or where they decided to change their prediction based on the reading.

Previewing (Vacca and Vacca 1996)

Although previewing can take many forms, Vacca and Vacca suggest that the teacher lead students through these procedures:

1. Read the title and convert it to a question.

2. Read the introduction, summary, and questions. What seem to be the main points?

3. Read the headings and subheadings and convert each to a question.

4. Read any print in special type.

5. Look at all visuals.

FLEXIBLE GROUPING IN READING • HOW-TO EXPLANATIONS OF READING STRATEGIES

Scholastic Professional Books, 1998

Picture Walk

1. Provide students with a copy of the story.

2. They look at the pictures.

3. Then they tell what they think the story will be about based on their picture walk.

4. Students read the story.

TEACHING STRATEGIES FOR DURING READING

The during-reading part of the lesson provides time for students to engage with the text, with or without teacher guidance. Given the range of reading achievement in any classroom, you need to use a variety of strategies to support all learners. Here are six during-reading activities that can provide the necessary support.

Cut-Apart (Opitz 1993)

The cut-apart is a story that has been divided into enough sections so that every student or small group has a part to read. This strategy enables all students to read a single story successfully, develops fluency through repeated reading, enhances listening comprehension, and provides for purposeful oral reading. I have found that this strategy works especially well with cumulative narrative text and text with specific parts for students to read.

1. Photocopy the selection.

2. As you read the selection, look for logical stopping points and mark them.

3. Look through the whole selection to make sure that you have created enough parts for each person or small group to have a section.

4. Cut the selection apart, mounting each part on oak tag. You may also want to list the title, author, and illustrator on a separate card. You could use this card to begin the story.

5. Number each part. Even though there may be more text in some sections, mounting each on the same-size paper will ensure that no student feels singled out.

6. Explain the procedure. I say something like this: "Today you're all going to read a different part of our story. I have put the different parts on these cards. The number on the card lets you know where your part fits. After I pass out the cards, you need to practice reading your part silently. Read it as many times as you can before you share it with the rest of the class. I'll be walking around to help. "

7. Pass out the cards. At times it won't matter who gets a given card; at other times you may want to give students specific cards to ensure successful reading.

8. Students sit in a circle in numerical order. Begin by reading the title and have each student read in turn. Ask the listeners to visualize what is happening in the story.

9. Discuss the selection.

CUMULATIVE NARRATIVE TEXT SUGGESTIONS

Patricia Polacco, *In Enzo's Gardens*
Margaret Dunphy, *Here Is the Wetland*
Margaret Dunphy, *Here Is the Tropical Rainforest*
Verna Aardema, *Bringing the Rain to Kapiti Plain*

Cooperative Reading Activity (CRA) (Opitz 1992)

This activity involves chunking informational text. It enables all learners to read a common expository passage and identify important information.

1. Identify a selection that is already divided by headings. Make sure that each section is about the same length so students finish about the same time.

2. Assign students to groups of four for each section.

3. Prepare copies of each section, one for each person.

4. Pass out record-keeping forms (page 111) so students can record important information.

5. Explain the procedure. I have found the following successful: "Today four of you will be reading one part of the story. When you have finished reading your part, write or underline three ideas you think the others in your group should know. Then, with your group members, decide on the three most important ideas. Write these on a chart and be ready to share your chart with the rest of the class."

6. Students read and write, both individually and in their groups.

7. Groups share their charts with the class.

INFORMATIONAL TEXT SUGGESTIONS

Judy Donnelly, *The Titanic Lost. . . and Found*
Robert Snedded, *What Is a Bird?*
Colin Threadgill, *Animal Homes*

My name _____

My section _____

Scholastic Professional Books, 1998

Genre Study

In this activity, students read different titles relating to the same genre. This enables all learners to contribute to the same theme regardless of their achievement levels.

1. Decide how you will group students.

2. Choose the genre you want students to learn and locate titles that provide "just right" material for each group.

3. Create a large matrix on which the groups can list their titles and make notations.

4. Introduce the genre to the class. I have found that a whole class read aloud facilitates this process. Discuss the book, pointing out features that are common to this type of genre. For example, if you focus on folktales, you might want to point out the use of repetition, characters with magical powers, trickery, and magic objects.

5. Show the class the matrix and have a volunteer write the title and the characteristics evident in the book you read aloud.

6. Introduce the books students will read.

7. Students read, and each group fills in the class matrix.

TIP: A variation of this is an author study in which children read books by the same author.

For titles, consult the references in Appendix B. See especially Campbell-Hill 1995; Peterson and Eeds 1990; and titles listed in *More Kids' Favorite Books* (1995).

Text Sets

Text sets are sets of books related to a common element or topic. In this activity, each student may read a different book related to the topic. Like genre studies, this activity enables all children to read about the same topic regardless of their achievement levels.

1. Identify the topic you want students to explore.

2. Identify students' general achievement levels.

3. Determine the size and number of groups.

4. Select books for each group that relate to the topic.

5. Tell students what they will be doing and have them read silently. Provide help as needed.

6. Groups tell about their books. Students in different groups tell how the information in their books is alike and different.

TEXT SETS

Alphabet
Max Grover, *The Accidental Zucchini*
Flora McDonnell, *Flora McDonnell's A B C*
Chuck Murphy, *Alphabet Magic*
Diana Pomeroy, *Wildflower A B C*
Fulvio Testa, *A Long Trip to Z*

Gardening
Douglas Florian, *Vegetable Garden*
Miela Ford, *Sunflower*
Henry Cole, *Jack's Garden*
Anita Lobel, *Alison's Zinnia*
Chris Peterson, *Harvest Year*

Shapes
Cathryn Falwell, *Shape Space*
Suse MacDonald, *Sea Shapes*
Eve Merriam, *The Hole Story*
Dayle Dodds, *The Shape of Things*
Max Grover, *Circles and Squares Everywhere!*

Single Title, Varied Mode (Cooper 1995)

In this approach, students read one title in several ways. This strategy provides the varying levels of support that different children need.

1. Choose the title students will read.

2. Determine the amount of support you will need to provide students for successful reading. Independent reading is appropriate for those for whom the book is just right and who want to read alone. Collaborative reading works for students who shouldn't experience too much difficulty but would like to read together just the same. Teacher guided will help children most likely to experience difficulty with much of the text. Recorded version is useful for students who learn by listening.

3. Group children according to needed support.

4. Children silently read a specified portion of the book.

5. The whole class completes the same type of activity, such as writing a summary in their literature response logs.

Ann Cameron, *More Stories Julian Tells*
Patrick Catling, *The Chocolate Touch*
Lois Lowry, *Number the Stars*

Paired Reading (Greene 1970)

In paired reading, students work with partners to read a text. A benefit of this approach is that it provides students with meaningful oral reading practice and helps develop fluency in a nonthreatening way. I have found this strategy to be especially helpful when the text is divided into two parts.

1. Explain to students that for the day's reading they will be reading with partners. Pair children who are less fluent with students who are more fluent.

2. With a volunteer, model how students should do their reading. Sitting side by side, one child reads orally while the other follows along or listens. When finished reading a section, the reader tells what has been read. The partners take turns reading and listening.

SUGGESTED TITLES

Betty Birney, *Pie's in the Oven*
Arnold Lobel, *Fables*
Jacqueline McQuale, *Good Times With Teddy Bear*
Angela Medearis, *Rum-a-tum-tum*
Laura Numeroff, *Two for Stew*

AFTER-READING TEACHING STRATEGIES

This phase of the lesson provides students with an opportunity to respond to the reading. It also enables students to reflect on their reading and to extend their comprehension. Clearly, all learners should be provided with these opportunities if they are to become stronger readers. Here are ten ways to have students respond to reading.

Class mural

Students express their understanding through art and also develop social skills.

1. Group students by four. Assign each group a scene from the story.

2. Group members work together to illustrate their scene.

3. Each group contributes its illustrations to a class mural.

Choral reading

This activity helps develop reading fluency while providing support for less able readers.

1. Place students in groups and provide each group with a part of the story.

2. Each group practices reading its part in unison.

3. Each group reads its part in turn to retell the story.

Comparison/Contrast

This activity helps students see likenesses and differences among characters or stories.

1. After reading a story with two main characters, draw a Venn diagram on the board. Label the left and right parts of the diagram with the names of the two characters. Label the center "Both."

2. Students discuss how the characters are alike and different. Place like characteristics in the middle of the diagram and the differences on the left and right.

Drama

1. After students have read a story, allow them time to reenact it.

2. Choose one student to be the narrator and have that student begin to retell the story. As students hear their character mentioned, they act out their part.

K-W-L (Ogle 1986)

Making a K-W-L chart offers students an opportunity to reflect on what they know about a subject and to identify what they learn after reading about it. Refer to page 108 for an explanation of this procedure.

Literature Response Logs

There are many ways students can respond to their reading in literature logs. Here are four.

1. Write a summary.

2. Do a character sketch of one or more characters. Students draw a stick

figure and place words around it to show how the character felt, acted, and thought.

3. Write three questions to use in a group discussion.

4. Write about the part they liked best or least and state why.

Puppet Theater

1. Divide students into groups based on the number of characters in the story.

2. Each student chooses a character.

3. Provide a variety of materials and time for students to create puppets to represent their characters.

4. Each group reenacts the story as a puppet show.

Readers Theater (Coger and White 1982)

This activity advances students' ability to improve oral-reading skills. It also calls for students to interpret the text and compose a script.

1. Discuss with students how scripts are used to turn books into movies.

2. Show the class copies of scripts and model what it is that the actors actually read. Explain how they know when to read their parts.

3. Group students according to the number of characters in the story they have read. Have the groups rewrite the story in script form. Explain that they may need to create the role of a narrator.

4. Make copies of the scripts for each member of a group and have students practice reading their lines.

5. Each group reads its script for the class.

Retelling

This activity provides students with the opportunity to recall what they learned from a passage and to share information. There are many ways to have students retell a story. Here is one procedure.

1. Each student tells everything that he or she can remember.

2. While listening, make notes about the student's comprehension.

Sketch to Stretch (Short, Harste, and Burke 1996)

Students should know that texts can be interpreted in more than one way. This activity enables readers to use drawing as a way of sharing their interpretations.

1. Provide each student with the reading selection, paper, pencils, and crayons or markers.

2. Ask students to think about what they have read and to draw a sketch showing what the selection meant to them.

3. Form groups of four or five and ask students to share their sketches with one another. The group members first tell what they think a sketch represents. Then the artist states his or her interpretation.

4. Each group then selects one sketch to share. Once displayed, the class offers its interpretations before the group shares.

Annotated
Bibliography

W ant some additional ideas and insights? This appendix should
prove helpful. Some of the articles and books offer information
about how other teachers have used flexible grouping in their
classrooms. Other references provide more teaching strategies and activities
for various parts of your lessons. The list is by no means complete. View it as
a starter list and add your own titles to it!

ARTICLES

Cunningham, P., D. Hall, and M. Defee 1991. Non-ability grouped, multilevel instruction: A year in a first grade classroom. *The Reading Teacher* 44 (8): 566–71.

> Three first-grade teachers developed and implemented a reading program that was used in place of traditional ability grouping. All components of the program, including how the basal reader was used, are explained. The authors also present data showing the success of the program.

Flood, J., D. Lapp, S. Flood, and G. Nagel, 1992. Am I allowed to group? Using flexible patterns for effective instruction. *The Reading Teacher* 45 (8): 608–16.

> A brief historical overview of grouping and considerations for alternative grouping patterns. The major part of the article details how and why the authors used five different grouping patterns to help third graders read a folktale.

Logan, N., J. Rux, and E. Paradis, 1991. Profile of a heterogeneous grouping plan for reading. *Reading Horizons* 32 (2): 86–95.

> Tells how a fifth-grade teacher set up and managed heterogeneous groups through the use of whole-class and group books. Includes a sample management plan as well as factors that the teacher believed contributed to student success.

Keegan, S., and K. Shrake, 1991. Literature study groups: An alternative to ability grouping. *The Reading Teacher* 44 (8): 542–47.

> Two fourth-grade teachers tell about their transition from using traditional ability groups to literature study groups. Specific ideas, ranging from how to get started to how to grade individual performance, are included.

Pardo, L., and T. Raphael, 1991. Classroom organization for instruction in content areas. *The Reading Teacher* 44 (8): 556–65.

> Discusses how a third-grade teacher used a variety of grouping techniques to help students learn about communication. Several activities used throughout the communication unit are listed and explained.

Reutzel, D. R., and R. Cooter, 1991. Organizing for effective instruction: The reading workshop. *The Reading Teacher* 44 (8): 548–54.

> Offers a framework for teaching reading via a workshop approach. Three cases of teachers using the workshop with and without traditional ability groups are also presented.

Wiggins, R. 1994. Large group lesson/small group follow-up: Flexible grouping in a basal reading program. *The Reading Teacher* 47 (6): 450–60.

> Shows how all third-grade teachers within one school implemented different grouping techniques in their classrooms. The authors explain how they used a basal reader in addition to other materials to create an effective language arts program.

Books

Caldwell, J., M. Ford, 1996. *Where Have All the Bluebirds Gone? Transforming Ability-Based Reading Classrooms.* Schofield, WI: Wisconsin State Reading Association.

  The first part provides a brief rationale for re-examining the way children are currently grouped during reading instruction. Part two presents different models that can be used in place of ability grouping. Part three, written by teachers of different grade levels, provides scenarios that describe a variety of grouping strategies.

Chambers, A. 1996. *Tell Me.* York, ME: Stenhouse.

  Some practical ways to get children talking about books. A framework is outlined as well as suggested questions.

Children's Choices 1995. *More Kids' Favorite Books.* Newark, DE: International Reading Association.

  An annotated listing of books selected by children. Books are organized according to stage of reading. Author/illustrator and title index.

Cohen, E. 1994. *Designing Groupwork: Strategies for the Heterogeneous Classroom.* 2nd ed. New York: Teachers College Press.

  Suggestions for successful groupwork. Includes several activities that can be used to help students learn how to work in groups. I have found this book to be an invaluable resource.

Craner, E., and M. Castle, 1994. *Fostering the Love of Reading: The Affective Domain in Reading Education.* Newark, DE: International Reading Association.

  Presents ideas for creating lifelong readers. Strategies for motivating readers, responding to reading, and developing reading programs focused on how students feel about reading are discussed at length.

Daniels, H. 1994. *Literature Circles: Voice & Choice in the Student-Centered Classroom.* York, ME: Stenhouse.

  A wealth of information to help get literature circles going. In addition to providing the background for the idea, the author presents specific suggestions for how to get started and how to schedule and manage groups. Sample materials are included as well as ideas for record keeping, evaluation, and grading. Primary through college teachers tell how they have used the ideas in their own classrooms.

Ellis, S., and S. Whalen, 1990. *Cooperative Learning: Getting Started.* New York: Scholastic.

  Essential information for the teacher who is new to cooperative learning. The authors give a brief rationale for using cooperative learning and specific suggestions for getting started. They also include some tried-and-true cooperative-learning techniques.

Fowler, J. and S. Newlon, 1995. *Quick and Creative Literature Response Activities: More Than 60 Sensational Hands-on Ideas.* New York: Scholastic.

  Provides several ways to encourage children to respond to literature. All ideas are teacher and child tested! Activities are primarily geared toward K–3.

Hearn, B. 1990. *Choosing Books for Children: A Commonsense Guide.* New York: Delacorte.
Offers suggestions for selecting and using literature along with recommended books for all age levels.

Hill, B., N. Johnson, K. Noe, 1995. *Literature Circles and Response.* Norwood, MA: Christopher-Gordon.
Presents several teachers' stories as they attempt to implement literature circles in the elementary school. Opens with a rationale for using literature circles and closes with an annotated bibliography of books that can be used for literature circles.

Maria, K. 1990. *Reading Comprehensional Instruction: Issues and Strategies.* New York: York Press.
An in-depth explanation of specific reading strategies to use before, during, and after reading. All explanations are accompanied by actual scripts illustrating the strategies in action with an entire class or group of students.

Musso, L. 1995. *25 Terrific Literature Activities.* New York: Scholastic.
Provides activities for all phases of reading—before, during, and after. Response activities are geared toward grades 4–8.

Peterson, R., M. Eeds, 1990. *Grand Conversations: Literature Groups in Action.* New York: Scholastic.
Gives a rationale for teaching with real books. Highlights teachers who use literature groups to show how the groups actually play out in different classrooms. The book closes with some suggested titles for kindergarten through sixth grade.

Roller, C. 1996. *Variability Not Disability.* Newark, DE: International Reading Association.
The author presents the argument that we will always have variability in our classrooms and that teachers need to know how to address it. The book shows how a reading/writing workshop can help teachers accommodate variability. There are detailed chapters on organization, set-up, and activities. Suggestions for record keeping are also included.

Stone, J. 1996. *Cooperative Learning Reading Activities.* San Clemente, CA: Kagan Cooperative Learning.
Lists and describes more than 100 cooperative activities that can be used with reading.

Yopp, H., and R. Yopp, 1996. *Literature-Based Reading Activities.* 2d ed. Needham Heights, MA: Allyn & Bacon.
Lists specific examples of activities that can be used before, during, and after reading. Also provides ideas for bookmaking and a list of Caldecott and Newbery books.

Children's Books Cited

Author	Title	Year	Location/Pub. Company
Aardema, Verna	Bringing the Rain to Kapiti Plain	1981	New York: Scholastic
Aardema, Verna	Why Mosquitoes Buzz in People's Ears	1975	New York: Dial
Asch, Frank	Just Like Daddy	1981	New York: Simon & Schuster
Barry, Hames, C. McClymont, and Glen Huser	Mystery Mazes	1993	Bothell, WA: Wright Group
Birney, Betty	Pie's in the Oven	1996	Boston: Houghton Mifflin
Butterworth, Nick	Busy People	1986	Cambridge: Candlewick
Cameron, Ann	The Stories Julian Tells	1981	New York: Random House
Cameron, Ann	More Stories Julian Tells	1986	New York: Random House
Carle, Eric	Have You Seen My Cat?	1987	New York: Scholastic
Catling, Patrick	The Chocolate Touch	1952	New York: Dell
Cleary, Beverly	Ramona and Her Mother	1979	New York: Morrow
Cole, Henry	Jack's Garden	1997	New York: Mulberry
Dodds, Dayle	The Shape of Things	1994	Cambridge: Candlewick
Donnelly, Judy	The Titanic Lost and Found	1987	New York: Random House
Dunphy, Margaret	Here Is the Wetland	1996	New York: Hyperion
Dunphy, Margaret	Here Is the Southwestern Desert	1995	New York: Hyperion
Dunphy, Margaret	Here Is the Tropical Rainforest	1994	New York: Hyperion
Falwell, Cathryn	Feast for 10	1993	New York: Scholastic
Falwell, Cathryn	Shape Space	1992	New York: Clarion
Florian, Douglas	Vegetable Garden	1991	San Diego: Harcourt
Ford, Miela	Sunflower	1995	New York: Greenwillow
Fox, Mem	Time for Bed	1993	San Diego: Harcourt
Galdone, Paul	The Three Wishes	1967	New York: McGraw-Hill
Galdone, Paul	The Monkey and Crocodile	1966	New York: Clarion
Grover, Max	The Accidental Zucchini	1997	San Diego: Harcourt

FLEXIBLE GROUPING IN READING • ANNOTATED BIBLIOGRAPHY
Scholastic Professional Books, 1998

Grover, Max	Circles and Squares Everywhere!	1996	San Diego: Harcourt
Lobel, Anita	Alison's Zinnia	1990	New York: Greenwillow
Lobel, Arnold	Fables	1980	New York: HarperCollins
Lowry, Lois	Number the Stars	1989	New York: Dell
MacDonald, Suse	Sea Shapes	1994	San Diego: Harcourt
McDonnell, Flora	Flora McDonnell's ABC	1997	Cambridge: Candlewick
Medearis, Angela	Rum-a-tum-tum	1997	New York: Holiday
McQuade, Jacqueline	Good Times With Teddy	1997	New York: Dial
Merriam, Eve	The Hole Story	1995	New York: Simon & Schuster
Mosel, Arlene	Tikki Tikki Tembo	1968	New York: Holt
Murphy, Chuck	Alphabet Magic	1997	New York: Simon & Schuster
Nodset, Joan	Who Took the Farmer's Hat?	1963	New York; Scholastic
Numeroff, Laura	Two for Stew	1996	New York: Simon & Schuster
Peterson, Chris	Harvest Year	1996	Honesdale, PA: Boyds Mills
Platt, Kin	Big Max	1963	
Polacco, Patricia	In Enzo's Splendid Garden	1997	New York: Philomel
Pomeroy, Diana	Wildflower ABC	1997	San Diego: Harcourt
Porter, George	An Interview with a Meteorologist	1989	New York: Silver-Burdett & Ginn
Root, Phyllis	The Hungry Monster	1997	Cambridge: Candlewick
Steptoe, John	Mufaro's Beautiful Daughters	1987	New York: Scholastic
Stevens, Janet	The House That Jack Built	1985	New York: Holiday
Sneeden, Robert	What Is a Bird?	1996	San Francisco: Sierra Club
Testa, Fulvio	A Long Trip to Z	1997	San Diego: Harcourt
Threadgill, Colin	Animal Homes	1996	New York: Crown

REFERENCES

Allington, R. 1977. "If they don't read much, how they ever gonna get good?"*Journal of Reading 21:* 57–61.

Allington, R. L. 1980. Teacher interruption behaviors during primary grade oral reading. *Journal of Educational Psychology* 72:371–72.

————1983. The reading instruction provided readers of differing reading ability. *Elementary School Journal 83*:255–65.

————1984. Content converage and contextual reading in reading groups. *Journal of Reading Behavior,16*:85–96.

Allington, R., and P. Cunningham, 1996. *Schools that Work.* New York: HarperCollins.

Anderson, R., E. Hiebert, J. Scott, and I. Wilkinson, 1985. *Becoming a Nation of Readers: The Report of the Commission on Reading.* Washington, D. C.: National Institute of Education.

Au, K., Mason, J. Scheu, 1995. *Literacy Instruction for Today.* New York: HarperCollins.

Barr, R. 1995. What research says about grouping in the past and present and what it suggests for the future. In *Flexible Grouping for Literacy in the Elementary Grades*, ed., M. Radenrich and L. McKay. Needham Heights, MA: Longwood.

Barr, R., and R. Dreeben, 1991. Grouping students for reading instruction. In *Handbook of Reading Research*, ed., R. Barr, M. Kamil, P. Mosenthal, P.D. Pearson, 2: 885–910. White Plains, NY: Longman.

Berghoff, B, and K. Egawa, 1991. No more "rocks": Grouping to give students control of their learning. *The Reading Teacher* 44 (8): 536–41.

Berliner, D. 1981. Academic learning time and reading achievement. In *Comprehension and Teaching: Research Reviews.* ed. J. Guthrie, 203–26. Newark, DE: International Reading Association.

Bettencourt, E. 1983. Effect of teacher enthusiasm on student on-task behavior and achievement. *American Educational Research Journal* 20: 435–50.

Bigelow, B. 1994. Getting off track: Stories from an untracked classroom. In*Rethinking Our Classrooms: Teaching for Quality and Justice.* ed. B. Bigelow, L. Christensen, S. Karp, B. Miner, & B. Peterson. Montgomery, AL: Rethinking Schools, Ltd.

Bridges, L. 1997. *Writing as a Way of Knowing.* York, ME: Stenhouse.

Brooks, E. 1996. *Just-Right Books for Beginning Readers.* New York: Scholastic.

Brophy, J. 1979. Teacher behavior and student learning. *Educational Leadership* 37: 33–8.

Calkins, L. 1995. *The Art of Teaching Writing.* 2d ed. Portsmouth, NH: Heinemann.

Clay, M. 1993. *An Observation Survey of Early Literacy Achievement* Portsmouth, NH: Heinemann.

Coger, L., and M. White, 1982. *Readers Theater Handbook: A Dramatic Approach to Literature.* Glenview, IL: Scott, Foresman.

Cohen, E. 1994. *Designing Groupwork: Strategies for the Heterogeneous Classroom.* New York: Teachers College Press.

Collins, C. 1980. Sustained silent reading periods: Effect on teachers' behaviors and students' achievements. *Elementary School Journal* 81 (2): 108–14.

Collins, J. 1986. Differential treatment in reading instruction. In *The Social Construction of Literacy.* ed. J. Cook-Gumerz. Cambridge, England: Cambridge University Press.

Cooper, J. D. 1995. Presentation at Colorado Council International Reading Association (February), Denver.

Cullinan, B. 1992. *Read to Me: Raising Kids Who Love to Read.* New York: Scholastic.

DeFord, D., C. Lyons, and G. Pinnell, eds. *Bridges to Literacy: Learning From Reading Recovery.* Portsmouth, NH: Heinemann.

DeStephano, J., J. Pepinsky, and T. Snaders, 1982. Discourse rules for literacy learning in a first-grade classroom. In *Communicating in the Classroom.* ed. L. C. Wilkinson, New York: Academic Press.

Dudley-Marling, C., and S. Stires, 1992. Including all students within a community of learners. *Reading Horizons* 32 (5): 361.

Duffelmeyer, F., A. K.ruse, D. Merkley, and S. Fyfe, 1994. Further validation and enhancement of the Names Test. *The Reading Teacher* 48 (2): 118–28.

Eder, D. 1981. Ability grouping as a self-fulfilling prophecy: A micro-analysis of teacher-student inter-action. *Sociology of Education* 54:151–61.

———1982. Differences in communicative styles across ability groups. In *Communicating in the Classroom.* ed. L. C. Wilkinson. New York: Academic Press.

———1983. Ability grouping and student's academic self-concepts: A case study. *The Elementary School Journal* 84: 149–61.

Farr, R., R. Carey, 1986. *Reading: What Can Be Measured?* Newark, DE: International Reading Association.

Farstrup, A., and M. Myers, 1996. *Standards for the English Language Arts.* Newark, DE and Urbana, IL: International Reading Association and National Council of Teachers of English.

Felmee, D., and D. Eder, 1983. Contextual effects in the classroom: The impact of ability groups on student attention. *Sociology of Education* 56: 77–87.

Fiderer, A. 1995. *Practical Assessments for Literature-Based Reading Classrooms.* New York: Scholastic.

Flood, J., D. Lapp, S. Flood, and G. Nagel, 1992. Am I allowed to group? Using flexible patterns for effective instruction. *The Reading Teacher* 45 (8): 608–16.

Gambrell, L. B., R. M.Wilson, W. N. Gnatt, 1981. Classroom observations of task-attending behaviors of good and poor readers. *Journal of Educational Research,* 74: 400–04.

Gambrell, L. 1984. How much time do children spend reading during teacher-directed reading instruction? In *Changing perspectives on research in reading/language processing and instruction.* ed. J. Niles and L. Harris. Thirty-third yearbook of the National Reading Conference. Rochester, NY: National Reading Conference.

Gamoran, A. 1992. Is ability grouping equitable? *Educational Leadership* 50 (2):11–7.

Gillett, J., and C. Temple, 1994. *Understanding Reading Problems: Assessmentand Instruction* 4th ed. New York: HarperCollins.

Good, T., and T. Beckerman, 1978. Time on task: A naturalistic study in sixth-grade classrooms. *Elementary School Journal* 78: 192–201.

Graves, D. 1994. *A Fresh Look at Writing.* Portsmouth, NH: Heinemann.

Gunning, T. 1996. *Creating Reading Instruction for All Children.* Needham Heights, MA: Allyn and Bacon.

Hallinan, M. 1984. Summary and implications. In *The Social Context of Instruction: Group organization and Group Processes.* , ed. P. Peterson, L. Wilkinson, and M. Hallinan.FL: Academic Press.

Harris, A. and E. Sipay, 1990. *How to increase Reading Ability: A Guide to Developmental & Remedial Methods* 9th ed.. White Plains, NY: Longman.

Haskins, R., T. Walden, and T. Ramey, 1983. Teacher and student behavior in high- and low-ability groups. *Journal of Educational Psychology* 75: 865–76.

Hastings, C. 1992. Ending ability grouping is a moral imperative. *Educational Leadership* 50 (2): 14.

Heller, M. 1995. *Reading-Writing Connections: From Theory to Practice* 2nd ed. White Plains, NY: Longman.

Herber, H. 1978. *Teaching Reading in Content Areas* 2nd ed.. Englewood Cliffs, NJ: Prentice-Hall.

Hiebert, E.H. 1983. An examination of ability grouping for reading instruction. *Reading Research Quarterly, 18*: 231–55.

Houser, M. 1992. Prologue: What Happens Before Alternative Groupings. *Reading Horizons* 31 (5): 343–348.

Johns, J. 1997. *Basic Reading Inventory*. 7th ed.. Dubuque, IA: Kendall/Hunt.

Johns, J., and S. Lenski, 1997. *Improving Reading: A Handbook of Strategies*. Dubuque, IA: Kendall/Hunt.

Johnson, and R. Johnson, 1987. *Learning Together and Alone: Cooperative, Conjunctive, and Individualistic Learning*. Englewood Cliffs, NJ: Prentice-Hall.

Jongsma, K. 1991. Grouping children for instruction: Some guidelines. *The Reading Teacher* 44 (8): 610–11.

Karweit, N. 1983. *Time on Task: A Research Review*. Report #332 (January). Baltimore: Center for Social Organization of Schools, Johns Hopkins University.

Kohn, A. 1996. *Beyond Discipline: From Compliance to Community*. Alexandria, VA: Association for Supervision and Curriculum Development.

Kulik, C. C., and J. A. Kulik, 1982. Effects of ability grouping on secondary students: A meta-analysis of evaluation findings. *American Educational Research Journal* 19: 415–28.

Langer, J. 1981. From theory to practice: A prereading plan. *Journal of Reading* 25 (2): 152–56.

Leinhardt, G., N. Zigmond, and W. Cooley, 1981. Reading instruction and its effects. *American Educational Research Journal* 18: 343–61.

Mann, M. 1960. What does ability grouping do to the self-concept? *Childhood Education (April)*: 357–60.

Manning, G., and M. Manning, 1984. What models of recreational reading make a difference? *Reading World 23* (4): 375–80.

McDermott, R. 1976. Kids make sense: An ethnographic account of the interactional management of success and failure in one first-grade classroom. Ph. D. dissertation, Stanford University.

Morrison, I. 1994. *Keeping It Together: Linking Reading Theory and Practice*. Bethell, WA: The Wright Group.

Norton, D. 1987. *Through the Eyes of a Child: An Introduction to Children's Literature*. Columbus, OH: Merrill.

Oakes, J. 1992. Can tracking research inform practice? *Educational Researcher* 21 (4): 12–21.

———1994. Tracking: Why schools need to take another route. In *Rethinking Our Classrooms: Teaching for Equity and Justice*. Montgomery, ed. B. Bigelow, L. Christensen, S. Karp, B. Miner, & B. Petersen AL: Rethinking Schools, Ltd.

Ogle, D. 1986. K-W-L: A teaching model that develops active reading of expository text. *The Reading Teacher* 39: 564–70.

Ohlausen, M. and Jepson, M., 1992. Lessons from Goldilocks: Somebody's been choosing my books but I can make my own choices now! *The New Advocate 5* (1).

Opitz, M. 1993. A cut-apart. *The Whole Idea* 3 (3): 12–13.

———1992. The cooperative reading activity: An alternative to ability grouping. *The Reading Teacher* 45 (9): 736–38.

———1994. *Learning Centers: Getting Them Started and Keeping Them Going*. New York. Scholastic.

———1995. *Getting the Most from Predictable Books*. New York, Scholastic.

Peterson, B. 1991. Selecting books for beginning readers and children's literature suitable for young readers. In *Bridges to Literacy: Learning from Reading Recovery* ed. D.E. DeFord, C.A. Lyons, and G.S. Pinnell (119–47). Portsmouth, NH: Heinemann.

Radencich, M., and L. McKay, 1995. *Flexible Grouping for Literacy in the Elementary Grades*. Needham Heights, MA: Allyn and Bacon.

Readence, J., T. Bean, and R. Baldwin, 1989. *Content Area Reading: An Integrated Approach*. Dubuque, IA: Kendall/Hunt.

Rhodes, L. and Dudley-Maring, C., 1988. *Readers and Writers With a Difference*. Portsmouth, NH: Heinemann.

Roller, C. 1996. *Variability Not Disability*. Newark, DE: International Reading Association.

Seltzer, D. 1976. A descriptive study of third-grade reading groups. *Dissertation Abstracts 36, 5811.* University Microfilms No. 76-6345.

Shannon, P. 1985. Reading instruction and social class. *Language Arts 62:* 604–13.

Short, K., J. Harste, and C. Burke, 1996. *Creating Classrooms for Authors and Inquirers* 2d ed. Portsmouth, NH: Heinemann.

Simons, H. and P. Ammon, 1989. Child knowledge and primerese text: Mismatches and miscues. *Research in the Teaching of English* 23 (4): 380–98.

Slavin, R. 1988. Cooperative learning and student achievement. In *School and Classroom Organization.* ed. R.E. Slavin Hillsdale, NJ: Erlbaum.

———1987. Ability grouping and student achievement in elementary schools: A best-evidence synthesis. *Review of Educational Research* 57 (3): 293–36.

Slavin, R., N. Karweit, and B. Wasik, 1994. *Preventing Early School Failure: Research, Policy, and Practice.* Needham Heights, MA: Allyn & Bacon.

Sorensen, A. and M. Hallinan, 1986. Effects of ability grouping on growth in academic achievement. *American Educational Research Journal* 23: 519–42.

Spear-Swerling, L. and R. Sternberg, 1996. *Off track: When Poor Readers Become Learning Disabled.* Boulder, CO: Westview Press.

Stanovich, K. 1986. Matthew effects in reading: Some consequences of individual differences in the acquisition of literacy. *Reading ResearchQuarterly* 21: 360–407.

Unsworth, L. 1984. Meeting individual needs through flexible within-class grouping of pupils. *The Reading Teacher (December):* 298–304.

Vacca, R. and J.. Vacca, 1996. *Content Area Reading,* 5th ed.. New York: HarperCollins.

Valencia, S. and D. Pearson, 1987. Reading assessment: A time for a change. *The Reading Teacher* 40 (8): 726–32.

Walmsley, S. and R. Allington, R. 1995. *No Quick Fix.* Newark, DE: International Reading Association.

Watson, D.1985. *Observing the Language Learner.* Newark, DE: International Reading Association.

Weinstein, R. 1976. Reading membership in first grade: Teacher behaviors and pupil experience over time. *Journal of Educational Psychology* 68: 103–16.

Wheelock, A. 1992. The case for untracking. *Educational Leadership* 50 (2):6–10.

———1992. *Crossing the Tracks: How "Untracking" Can Save America'sSchools.* New York: The New Press.

Yopp, H. 1995. A test for assessing phonemic awareness in young children. *The Reading Teacher* 49 [1]: 20–9.

Zaragoza, N. 1997. *Rethinking Language Arts: Passion and Practice.* New York: Garland.